Professional ... A Pro... **Guide**

Professional Conduct for Chartered Surveyors

A Practical Guide

Geoffrey Williams QC

Please note: References to the masculine include, where appropriate, the feminine.

Published by RICS Business Services Limited
a wholly owned subsidiary of
The Royal Institution of Chartered Surveyors
under the RICS Books imprint
Surveyor Court
Westwood Business Park
Coventry CV4 8JE
UK

No responsibility for loss occasioned to any person acting or refraining from action as a result of the material included in this publication can be accepted by the author or publisher.

ISBN 1 84219 129 2

Typeset in Great Britain by Columns Design Ltd, Reading
Printed in Great Britain by Martins the Printers, Berwick upon Tweed

Contents

Preface

Red tape is a constant frustration in a busy professional practice – but a necessary one. Unfortunately the public are increasingly sceptical of self-regulated professional values. The only way therefore that we can maintain our professional reputations is to define and publicise our professional values as Members of RICS and to discipline those Members who fall short of these exacting standards.

Defining professional values with sufficient precision to guide individual Members as to what actions are acceptable, and what actions are not, is not at all straightforward. Within the Ethics, Conduct and Consumer Protection Committee we strive to achieve a balance between brevity, intelligibility and precision in the rules which govern our Members whilst at all times making those rules relevant and as straightforward as possible for our Members to implement.

How refreshing it is, therefore, to see a book such as this written by an eminent lawyer giving practical advice on the interpretation and application of our rules.

This book is essential reading and reference material for all principals, sole practitioners and practice managers who employ Members of the RICS. It also provides an interesting and memorable refresher for our Members whose practice management obligations are taken care of by their employers – for we are a Members' organisation regulating each of our Members individually.

This book will also be interesting reading for clients of our Members to better understand the standards that we value and how we regulate ourselves.

Although this book is aimed at practitioners rather than APC candidates, it does nevertheless put the rules into a practical context in a way that APC candidates will undoubtedly find interesting and enlightening. I can think of no better preparation for the APC than a quick read of this book. Whilst this book is not a replacement for the Rules, it does introduce and explain the Rules in an accessible and easy-to-read manner with lots of examples and recommendations.

Finally, a point worth clarifying is that our rules apply to all Members of RICS and not just Chartered Surveyors. Therefore, the Rules apply just as much to Student Members, Probationers and Technical Members as they apply to our Chartered Surveyor Members.

Richard Mills FRICS, June 2004.

Solicitor.

Chairman of the Ethics, Conduct and
Consumer Protection Committee.

Introduction

These days it is widely accepted amongst professions that self-regulation is a privilege not a right.

For the privilege to be maintained it is essential that professional bodies are able to demonstrate that they regulate their Members in the public interest. A particular line of criticism is that professions 'look after their own'.

In my experience, this is not the case. Professionals tend to be harder on each other than is generally understood.

The respect of the public cannot be taken for granted. A profession must be able to demonstrate that it is taking steps to guard its reputation by requiring the highest ethical standards of its Members. Furthermore, those who lapse from those standards must be seen to be subject to proper and effective disciplinary process. Only by such measures can the public confidence be maintained.

The Royal Institution of Chartered Surveyors derives its powers in this area from the Royal Charter. This imposes upon the Institution an obligation to maintain and promote the usefulness of the profession to the public advantage.

To that end, Bye-Laws and Regulations have been promulgated so as to form the disciplinary framework for the profession. Members' obligations are precisely set out and Guidance Notes provide further amplification. All these materials are readily available to all Members.

However, many years have elapsed since a practical guide was written to accompany the core documents.

I was therefore very flattered to be asked by Steven Gould and Suzanne Phillips of RICS to set about the task of writing this book. It is my first foray into authorship and I have taken it to be a heavy responsibility.

It must be stressed that this book does not replace the need for all Members to read and digest the relevant Bye-Laws and Regulations. The aim of this book is to set those provisions into a practical context and I have concentrated on the areas which provide most of the subject matter for disciplinary proceedings at their various levels. As well as setting out what I believe to be the most important provisions, I have also attempted to aid the reader in developing an instinct for regulatory and conduct problems and I have set out some hints as to how these problems may be avoided. I have sought to give guidance as to the approaches to be adopted once problems have arisen, with particular emphasis on mitigating the penal consequences.

Members should also be aware that the Institution is only too willing to offer assistance in times of difficulty. Far too few Members take advantage of this opportunity often, regrettably, to their cost. Help is at hand and I hope this book contributes in such a way.

As well as thanking Steven and Suzanne for their inspiration, my thanks also go to Kathy Wiley and Heather Douglas for their production of the various drafts of my work. I am particularly indebted to Simon Buckler of the Professional Conduct Department of RICS who has brought his considerable experience and expertise to bear upon the more technical aspects. Any mistakes, however, are mine.

Geoffrey Williams QC

Conduct Unbefitting

Bye-Law 19(1) provides that 'every Member shall conduct himself in a manner befitting membership of the Institution'.

It is not by coincidence that this takes pride of place amongst the Bye-Laws.

The principle forms the bedrock of the system of self-regulation of Chartered Surveyors. It can fairly be said that practice in accordance with the spirit of this Rule is likely to ensure compliance with the range of Bye-Laws and Rules of Conduct that Chartered Surveyors undertake to abide by on admission to the profession.

What is 'Conduct Unbefitting'?

Many will take the view that as this is such a fundamental principle then it should be clearly defined. However, no precise definition is available despite various attempts having been made, particularly by other professions.

For instance, in the case of solicitors, there is authority to the effect that for a particular activity to amount to Conduct Unbefitting, then it must be behaviour that is either:

1

(1) disgraceful; or

(2) dishonourable; or

(3) liable to bring the profession into disrepute.

Various other approaches have been adopted in this and other professions over the years, but the modern approach is to consider it appropriate that a precise definition should be avoided.

Such an approach enables the profession to move with the times. Activities that may have been regarded as Conduct Unbefitting some years ago may be viewed more tolerantly these days, and indeed vice versa. For instance, racial or sexual harassment and discrimination is considered much more serious than hitherto.

This is reflected by the fact that in March 2002, the new Bye-Law 19(12) was introduced to the effect that:

> ' ... a Member shall not in the course of his professional business discriminate against any person on grounds of race, colour, culture, nationality, ethnic or national originals, religion, gender, marital status, sexual orientation or disability'.

Thus, discriminatory behaviour has become a specific conduct offence regardless of whether or not it can be termed 'Conduct Unbefitting'.

It is fair to say that conduct is unbefitting a Chartered Surveyor if a Professional Conduct Panel or Disciplinary Board considers it to be so in the context of all the facts of the case at the time in question.

The predecessor Bye-Law 19(1) stated that 'no Member shall conduct himself in a manner unbefitting a Chartered Surveyor'. The new wording is more positive and is more than a semantic difference. Rule 3 (under Conduct Regulation 27.1) relates to this Bye-Law and sets out what are described as 'core values'. Again these are expressed in deliberately wide terms and Members are expected to:

- act with integrity;

- always be honest;

- be open and transparent in all dealings;

- be accountable for all actions;

- know and act within their limitations;

- be objective at all times;

- treat others with respect;

- set a good example; and

- have the courage to make a stand.

Practice in accordance with these core values is mandatory, but they will of course be construed according to the facts of any particular case. They provide a framework for membership of a profession which depends for its reputation upon honourable conduct by its Members. They call for honesty, trustworthiness, proper standards of work, respectful behaviour and independence of mind.

Rule 3 also provides that the Chartered Surveyor, or indeed anyone acting on his behalf or upon his instructions, must not act in a manner which compromises or impairs, or is likely to compromise or impair, any of the following:

- the integrity of the Member;

- the reputation of the Institution, the surveying profession or other Members;

- the high standards of professional conduct expected of a Member;

- compliance with any code, standard or Practice Statement of the Institution or any statute in force at the time;

- the Member's duty to act in the legitimate interest of his client or employer subject to legal or similar constraints;

- a person's freedom to instruct a Member of his choice.

With respect to this Rule it is important to note that not only must the Member act accordingly, but so must his staff or agents. Again the definitions are wide and advisedly so.

It is inappropriate to construe these provisions according to their letter. Compliance with the spirit of these Rules is required and in particular an awareness of potential problems is essential.

Any serious lapse from the high ethical standards required of Chartered Surveyors can be expected to amount to Conduct Unbefitting. The lapse need not be the result of a positive action. Conduct Unbefitting can arise from, for instance, turning a blind eye in circumstances where positive action or communication is called for.

Accordingly, we find at the heart of the system of self-regulation an obligation not to fall below standards which are not precisely defined and should not be so defined. If, however, Members conduct themselves honestly and with professional propriety, they are most unlikely to fall foul of the Bye-Law and the Rule.

How far does this obligation extend?

Your private life

The obligation to behave in a manner befitting membership of the Institution does not cease when the office is closed.

It is no defence to a Charge of Conduct Unbefitting that the conduct complained of arose outside the scope of professional practice. Public and private misbehaviour can affect the membership of the profession. For instance, if a Chartered Surveyor is convicted of a serious offence by a Criminal Court, it is likely that there will be more publicity than would ordinarily be the case by virtue of the fact that the Defendant is a professional person. The reputation of the profession then suffers in consequence. This is particularly the case when the conviction relates to the integrity of the Member.

A Professional Conduct Panel has recently dealt with a Member who threatened to slash the tyres on a lady's car and used foul language in the process. He maintained that he should not be disciplined as the incident took place in a private car park. This attempt at a defence failed.

Specific examples

It will already be clear that there is no precise definition of unbefitting conduct. Therefore there can be no definitive list of examples of such conduct.

Accordingly, it cannot be assumed that because a transgression is not referred to below, then all is well.

However, the following are examples of what may be considered to be Conduct Unbefitting a Chartered Surveyor.

- Any dishonesty – whether or not resulting in a criminal conviction.

- Misapplication of clients' funds – whether for the Member's benefit or otherwise.

- Refusing to enter into an undertaking required by a disciplinary body of the Institution.

- Breaching an undertaking given to the Institution or any other third party.

- Giving false and/or misleading information to the Institution or any third party.

- Criminal convictions for serious offences or repeated convictions for minor offences.

- Failure to communicate or co-operate with the Institution either in the course of an investigation of a client complaint, or in circumstances where the Institution has generated its own inquiry into regulatory matters.

- Wilful failure to maintain compliant Professional Indemnity Insurance.

- Wilful failure to comply with the Members Accounts' Regulations.

- The writing of aggressive or abusive correspondence to any party.

- Discrimination either direct or indirect on the grounds of race, religion, gender, sexual orientation or disability.

- Culpable failure to comply with a proper direction of the Institution.

- Acting improperly in a conflict of interest situation.

- Improperly divulging confidential information.

The above list represents types of conduct held to be in breach of this Bye-Law and is neither exhaustive nor expressed in any order of seriousness.

Practical aspects

A Member may face a Charge of Conduct Unbefitting before a Professional Conduct Panel or Disciplinary Board as a result of acts or omissions which will be set out clearly in the Charge. The Member will know that it is being alleged that he has breached this Bye-Law and will have a clear picture of the case against him.

The Bye-Law is not a stand-alone provision. Charges of unbefitting conduct can also attach to alleged breaches of other Rules of Conduct. This would apply in situations where the breach of the other Rule, e.g. failure to maintain compliant Professional Indemnity Insurance was considered by the Institution to be particularly serious – in other words an aggravated breach.

Consequences

Where a Member is found to have been guilty of unbefitting conduct, then inevitably a very serious view will be taken of it by a Disciplinary Board. Membership of the Institution will be at risk.

Self-preservation

The answer of course lies in the Member's own ethical standards. The vast majority of Chartered Surveyors go through their professional careers upholding the highest standards of professional conduct.

However, from time to time it is inevitable that in the course of practice problems will arise which could lead a Member to conduct himself in a manner unbefitting a Member of the Institution. Very often these problems arise through no fault of the Member and in circumstances which he could not reasonably have foreseen.

The key defence mechanism is the ability to recognise when a potential problem arises and then act appropriately in dealing with it.

An honourable and honest approach to the issue is likely to avoid unbefitting conduct.

It must be carefully borne in mind that when such a predicament arises the Member finds it difficult to apply the same degree of objectivity that is normally achieved in day-to-day practice. Therefore, it is usually insufficient to rely on your own judgement and the golden rule is to seek help.

Such help can come from various sources. The first port of call may be a professional colleague within the Member's own practice, but the same objectivity problem may apply. Professional colleagues in other practices may also be glad to help and can bring a fresh mind to the situation.

By far the best approach is to seek help from the Institution itself. Some may be surprised at this advice. It may be thought akin to venturing into the lion's den. Nothing could be further from the truth. The Institution has a specialist team who would be happy to give confidential advice.

When seeking such advice it is essential that all the facts are placed before the Institution so that informed advice can be given. If the advice is followed, then the best possible defence to a Charge of Conduct Unbefitting has been obtained.

Doing nothing is never an option. Hoping that a problem will go away rarely if ever leads to that result – a positive approach is essential.

A Member facing such difficulties must never take steps to attempt to cover his tracks. This is likely to involve dishonest conduct and simply serves to make a bad situation much worse.

The discovery of Conduct Unbefitting by others

As has been seen, Members are exhorted to 'have the courage to make a stand'. The Guidance issued by RICS with respect to its Rule of Conduct makes it plain that a Member must be prepared to act if he suspects a risk to

9

safety or malpractice of any sort. Whilst this may fall short of a positive obligation to report misconduct in others, it is suggested that it is in the interests of both the public and the system of self-regulation, for Members to refer to the Institution in cases where they are of the view that a fellow Member may be guilty of misconduct.

This can, of course, be an unpleasant duty and courage is certainly required, but the interests referred to above are paramount.

Furthermore, a Member must never be seen to be complicit in the misconduct of another and turning a blind eye is inappropriate.

There are specific Bye-Laws which operate on this subject outside the scope of 'Conduct Unbefitting'.

Bye-Law 19(10) provides that every Member must disclose to the Institution promptly the details of any other Member who may be in breach of the Regulations with respect to Professional Indemnity Insurance and the keeping of accounts.

Furthermore, Bye-Law 19(11) provides that every Member must disclose to the Institution promptly in writing, that either he, or to the best of his information, knowledge and belief, any other Member, has been charged with or convicted of a criminal offence involving embezzlement, theft, corruption, fraud or dishonesty of any kind, or any other criminal offence carrying on first conviction the possibility of a custodial sentence.

Compliance with these Bye-Laws is mandatory and any breach need not be characterised by the term 'Conduct

Unbefitting'. Members who consider that they may be under a duty to report under these provisions may well wish to seek legal or other professional advice of their own in the first instance.

The position of an employed Member who discovers potential Conduct Unbefitting by his employer Member is obviously difficult. In these circumstances, the employee should, in the first instance, confront the employer in which event a perfectly acceptable explanation may be given.

Having taken this step, if doubts remain, then the employee should contact the Institution for guidance. It will be readily understood that the employee Member will wish to protect his own position.

Members should also note that a specific responsibility is imposed by Bye-Law 20. This involves a broad definition of the term 'Member' and imposes a responsibility for any conduct contravention by any person (Member or otherwise) for whom the Member in question has responsibility. In other words, there is a vicarious responsibility for the conduct of others within the Member's organisation. There is, however, a defence if the Member can show that without any fault on his part he had no reason to be aware, and was not in fact aware, of any such contravention and that he had prior to the contravention, taken such steps as were reasonable to ensure that the contravention would not be committed. Two points are of note:

(1) The onus is on the Member to establish this defence.

(2) If the offence is established, the Member may be relieved in whole or in part of responsibility for the

contravention. Thus, even if the Member establishes the defence, he may not be exonerated. All will depend upon the particular facts of the case.

A Member's own Conduct Unbefitting

There is no positive Rule requiring a Member to report himself to the Institution. Bear in mind, however, that bad news travels fast. It is far better for the Institution to hear what may be bad news from the Member himself than from a third party. Self-reporting represents very significant mitigation. It will not prevent the Institution, where appropriate, offering help and guidance and may serve to dispose of the problem altogether. Convictions are matters of public record and the Institution is likely to find out about them in any event. Frankness in all dealings with the Institution is essential.

Lifelong learning

Bye-Law 19(8) requires Members to undertake Lifelong Learning ('LLL') which was formerly termed 'Continuing Professional Development'. Furthermore, Members are obliged to provide the Institution with evidence of compliance.

Lifelong Learning means the systematic maintenance, improvement and broadening of professional knowledge, understanding and skill, and the development of professional and technical duties throughout the practitioner's working life. This requirement operates in both the interests of the public and the Member.

Self-regulation of all professions depends upon the confidence of the public being maintained. Such confidence must exist both with regard to the professional conduct and the professional competence of Members.

Members' businesses are enhanced by the acquisition and development of skills throughout the Member's career.

The nature of the obligation

Conduct Rule 37 provides that a Member must complete a minimum of 60 hours LLL comprising Qualifying

Activity in every period of three consecutive years. A minimum of ten hours LLL must be carried out each year.

As the term suggests, LLL must be pursued throughout the Member's career and the extent of the obligation does not decrease with seniority.

Qualifying Activities

For hours to count, they must be spent in the pursuit of a 'Qualifying Activity'.

LLL involves commitment in both terms of time and finance. It is therefore essential that it is properly targeted so as to fulfil the professional obligation.

The term 'Qualifying Activity' is defined in Rule 35 and can be paraphrased as meaning the study of:

(a) the theory and practice of surveying;

(b) surveying topics relating to a Member's current or potential occupation;

(c) topics relating to the acquisition of personal or business skills; and/or

(d) such other topics considered by the Institution to relate appropriately to a Member's management or business efficiency by one or more of the following means:

   (i) attendance at conferences, workshops, seminars, etc;

   (ii) distance learning;

(iii) attendance at meetings, working groups, etc;

(iv) private study and pre-course reading in a structured form – this cannot amount to more than two-thirds of the total required hours;

(v) job development and experience-based learning;

(vi) preparation for publication of technical work and research and first delivery of presentations to other professionals;

(vii) additional activities, e.g. acting as an assessor or external examiner.

How are the hours calculated?

Rule 37 provides that where a Member attends a formal event, then the maximum time attributable to the Qualifying Activity shall be the duration from the opening to the closing of that event calculated to the nearest half hour, or from the commencement to the completion of other informal activities.

Needless to say, where the attendance is only for part of the Qualifying Activity, then only the time attended is counted, and time spent administering a Qualifying Activity does not count at all.

Newly admitted Chartered Surveyors

There is a provision with relation to Chartered Surveyors qualifying on or after 1 September 2004. Their learning objectives must include business management knowledge, skills and/or understanding. Hours devoted to study and examinations will count as a Qualifying Activity.

The record keeping requirement

Members are responsible for keeping their own records leading to compliance with the obligation. A failure in relation to either requirement will amount to a conduct offence.

The record must be kept in writing and in a prescribed form.

The Institution carries out random checks upon compliance and when called upon to do so, a Member must submit a copy of his records within 28 days of the request.

New obligations with respect to record keeping take effect from 1 January 2004 and are as follows.

(1) Every Member must maintain (at least) on an annual basis a record of his learning objectives, the date on which they were last recorded or updated, and the manner in which he intends to meet those objectives.

(2) With minor exceptions, Chartered Surveyors admitted on or after 1 September 2004 must include within the objectives, business management skills.

(3) Members admitted on or after 1 January 2004 must transmit their records electronically when called upon to do so.

The required records must be kept for at least three years after the Qualifying Activity has been undertaken.

Practical problems with compliance

The Institution readily appreciates that in certain circumstances Members will have difficulties in complying with their LLL obligation.

If this proves to be the case, then a Member may apply in writing for a waiver of this requirement.

The Chief Executive of the Institution has a discretion to grant a waiver in response to an application based on the grounds of:

- redundancy;

- ill health;

- pregnancy;

- any exceptional reason.

The latter ground confers a wide discretion, but Members should assume that the word 'exceptional' will be construed restrictively. Matters such as pressure of work which arise in the life of any professional would not, it is thought, be generally regarded as exceptional.

Waiver Applications will be considered entirely on their own merits and a sympathetic view would be taken in particular of the specific grounds above.

If Members are uncertain about their positions, then contact should be made with the CPD Library and Information Officer in the Education and Training Department.

The Institution will also assist with the supply of documentation for record keeping. The use of this documentation is highly recommended as it leaves no doubt that records are being kept in proper form.

Members will occasionally be in genuine doubt as to whether or not a proposed activity will count towards the

LLL obligation. In such circumstances, assumptions should be avoided and guidance obtained from the Institution.

Upon receipt of details of the proposed Activity, the CPD Library and Information Officer will give clear guidance as to whether or not it counts. Therefore, be absolutely clear about the nature of the Activity when communicating with the Institution.

A constructive approach is adopted by the Institution and flexibility will be permitted as long as the spirit of the Regulation is being complied with.

Furthermore, advice on this subject is published in RICS *Business* and on the Institution's website. There is ample help available.

Monitoring and disciplinary sanctions

Aside from the random monitoring process, instances arise where the Institution has reason to believe that a Member has not complied with his obligation.

The first step will be for the Institution to request an explanation from the Member and there is, of course, an obligation in conduct to co-operate with the Institution.

Cases of non-compliance are generally referred to Professional Conduct Panels which may (if the case is regarded as sufficiently serious) refer the matter on to a Disciplinary Board.

Naturally in cases of non-compliance, the best mitigation that can be put forward is that the default has been remedied before disciplinary consideration is given to it.

Disciplinary sanctions must be anticipated in cases of non-compliance. Also, a defaulting Member is likely to be required to enter into an undertaking with the Institution as to future compliance with the hours and record keeping requirements and possibly with regular reports upon progress. As discussed elsewhere, a refusal to enter into such an undertaking or a breach of it is likely to be regarded as Conduct Unbefitting, in which event much more serious sanctions are likely to be applied.

Self-preservation

The following approach is recommended.

- Take steps to understand your obligation – particularly with respect to the Qualifying Activity.

- Before committing yourself to any such Activity, be sure that the hours will count.

- Make use of the information provided by the Institution through a number of sources.

- Do not hesitate to discuss with the Institution in any case of doubt.

- Adopt a strategic approach – spread the Qualifying Activity evenly throughout the relevant period, and remember that a minimum of ten hours must be carried out every calendar year. Do not find yourself in a position of having to achieve too many hours within a truncated period at the end of the three years.

- Be meticulous in your record keeping and preferably use the documentation issued by the Institution.

- Remember your requirement to keep a record of your participation over the last three years, and the requirement to record your learning objectives.

- Make a written Application for a Waiver if appropriate, but do not assume it will be granted until you have received written confirmation.

- Be pro-active in your communications with the Institution, and certainly reply fully to all requests for explanations.

- To obtain the greatest benefit from LLL, a Member will need to treat it as an opportunity and not as a burden. Competition within the profession is fierce and the enhancement of skills has a direct benefit, both to the Member's practice and the reputation of the profession.

Disciplinary structures and procedures

A Member in breach of a Bye-Law or Rule of Conduct can expect to find himself subject to the disciplinary process of the Institution.

This can be triggered by either a complaint or allegation made by a client or other third party or alternatively as a result of information obtained by the Institution itself, for instance breaches of the Rules with respect to Accounts, Indemnity Insurance, Lifelong Learning, etc.

The Investigation

The Investigation is the first stage of the process. It is carried out by officers employed by RICS, many of whom have specialist knowledge of particular fields of activity.

The Investigation is a written process and is dealt with by correspondence to the Member. There is a duty in conduct to co-operate fully with such enquiries.

When corresponding, the Institution will clearly set out the nature of the complaint or allegation and a response will be requested within a set period of time. Should a Member need more time then he should submit a written request to which reasonable consideration will be given.

Of course in many cases, the Investigation concludes at an early stage and in favour of the Member. However, in those cases falling outside this category, and where the Institution is satisfied that there has been on the face of it a regulatory breach, then a formal letter will be written to the Member confirming that the matter will be investigated in accordance with the Bye-Laws and Rules. The Member is notified of his rights and also of the powers of the Institution. Again the nature of the complaint or allegation should be made perfectly clear.

The disciplinary functions of the Institution are exercised by:

- Professional Conduct Panels (PCPs);

- Disciplinary Boards;

- Appeal Boards; and

- The Chief Executive – who has certain powers delegated to him.

The functions and procedures of each will be discussed individually.

Professional Conduct Panels

A PCP is a first instance body which often provides the first opportunity for an oral hearing of the matter in question.

PCP's consist of at least five members, one of whom must be a lay member, i.e. not a Chartered Surveyor.

Chairmen are specifically appointed and all surveyor members of PCPs will be distinguished Members of the profession.

In cases where the Chairman considers that specialist assistance is required, then a suitable person (professional or lay) can be co-opted.

Referral to a PCP

The first stage is the formal notice to the Member referred to above. It invites the Member's written observations in advance of the hearing.

The Member will be told that he has the right to appear in person before a PCP and be represented by a lawyer or other person of his choice. If he does not wish to attend, then the hearing will proceed in his absence.

At such hearings, the Institution is usually represented by a member of staff and both the Institution and the Member can call witnesses subject to the discretion of the Chairman.

A PCP actually has the power to require a Member to attend at the hearing, to require the Member to produce relevant documents and to request the attendance of witnesses.

Furthermore, there is a power to call for additional information or evidence from either party, in which event the Member must have sufficient opportunity to consider and address this information before a decision is taken.

Hearings almost inevitably are heard at the RICS headquarters in London, but the Honorary Secretary may decide that a disciplinary body can be convened outside the UK if the Member so lives and practises his profession and it will help a fair hearing.

PCP hearings take place in private.

The powers of a PCP

If a PCP finds that the Charges before it have not been made out, then the Member will be so informed and the matter will have reached its conclusion.

However if there is a Finding that a Member has been in breach of a Bye-Law or Rule, then the PCP may do one, or more, of the following.

(1) Issue a caution against repetition of the conduct in question.

(2) Reprimand the Member.

(3) Severely Reprimand the Member.

(4) Impose a fine not exceeding £1,000 per contravention

(5) Require the Member to give an undertaking to either:

    (a) refrain from continuing or repeating the conduct in question;

    (b) take remedial action within a particular time limit;

    (c) refrain from practising surveying of the description specified in the undertaking, or to refrain from such practising except in accordance with prescribed conditions; or

    (d) where the contravention is the result of conduct of a person for whom the person is responsible, use best endeavours to ensure that the conduct in question ceases.

There is no Appeal from a decision of a PCP.

There is also a power to refer the subject matter to a Disciplinary Board. This is often exercised in cases of particular complexity or seriousness.

Before exercising any of its powers (including the power to refer), a PCP may take into account the disciplinary record of a Member.

Where a PCP finds a Member in breach, then the appropriate note is made on the personal record file which will also detail the penalty imposed or the undertaking required.

Unless the PCP directs otherwise, its Finding and Decision will be published in RICS *Business* and on the Institution's website and publication will include such details of the matter as the PCP thinks fit.

The PCP also has discretion to order that its finding and decision be notified to any other newspaper or publication.

A PCP also has powers to order costs either in favour of, or payable by, the Institution depending upon the result.

PCP hearings can be adjourned where necessary and this power is often exercised to allow the Member more time to put its house in order.

Temporary suspension

Bye-Law 21(5) gives the Institution a discretion to suspend a Member temporarily or require the Member to refrain from practising surveying of one or more specific descriptions and/or to use his best endeavours to ensure that his practice so refrains pending full Inquiry. This power will not be exercised until due notice has been given to the Member inviting him to make written submissions prior to the hearing. However, if the Chief Executive believes that this power should be exercised immediately in the public interest, then he may proceed accordingly with the approval of two of the Chairmen and/or Vice-chairmen of the PCP.

Principles of sentencing adopted by the PCPs

The least severe penalty is a Caution. This is normally reserved for cases where the Member has acted through inexperience, his breach has been minor and repetition is thought to be unlikely.

The next level of penalty – Reprimands and Severe Reprimands are the least that can normally be expected in cases of breach.

When considering imposing a fine, a PCP will seek information concerning the financial position of the Member, and will take into account any loss by the client and any benefit gained by the Member from his breach.

Undertakings are required with a view to seeking the practical resolution of the matter at issue. A time limit will be imposed and normally undertakings will contain a statement that if they are breached, then there will be an automatic referral to a Disciplinary Board.

The question of publication will be considered below.

Disciplinary Boards

Disciplinary Boards deal with the most serious cases. In contrast with PCPs, the hearings take place in public.

The Board consists of between three and five persons including at least one lay member, a Chartered Surveyor Chairman and at least one technical member if the Respondent Surveyor is a technical member who is not prepared to waive this provision.

Another distinguishing factor of Disciplinary Boards is the presence of a Legal Assessor. In practice, this is invariably a Barrister of some experience. If the Legal Assessor is called upon to give legal advice, then this is given in the hearing so that all concerned may have the opportunity to make Submissions upon that advice.

The Legal Assessor normally retires with the Board members. If he has been asked for advice during the retirement, he will repeat that advice in open hearing when the Board returns.

If a case has been referred by a PCP, then the Disciplinary Board will not contain a member who sat on the PCP.

The first formal stage in the process of Proceedings before Disciplinary Boards is that a document termed a 'Charges Letter' is served upon the Member by the Institution. This letter will have been drafted by the Institution's Disciplinary Solicitor who will have had sight of all relevant papers. He will bring his own discretion to bear upon the drafting, but will not stray outside the areas of conduct which have been set out in correspondence to the Member and/or aired before a PCP.

The Charges Letter will also contain practical information with respect to the hearing and be delivered at least 28 days before the hearing takes place.

The Member will be invited to submit a written Defence and disclose the identity of any representative he may instruct. It will be made clear that should the Member not attend before the Board, then the hearing may take place in his absence.

The Letter will also inform the Member that the Disciplinary Solicitor must serve his bundle of documentary evidence upon the Member at least 14 days before the hearing. In practice, the Disciplinary Solicitor will prepare a bundle commencing with the Charges Letter and paginated copies of all the documents upon which he relies and which are referred to in an Index.

Enclosed with the Charges Letter will be notes of the procedure to be followed at the hearing.

Again the Member is entitled to appear personally and/or by a representative and evidence can be called by both the Disciplinary Solicitor and the Member.

A shorthand writer attends the hearing and makes a full note of all that is said – this is of particular importance should there be an Appeal.

As with PCPs, cases are occasionally adjourned for various reasons with the Board having a full discretion.

Once the case is concluded, the Board retires in private to consider its findings on the allegations. If they have been admitted at the outset, then an immediate finding will have been made. If the decision is adverse to the Member, then he has the opportunity to address the Board in mitigation.

The Board will be made aware of the Member's disciplinary record once adverse findings have been made.

The Board will retire and then return with its decisions on penalty, costs and publication. Reasons will be given and rights of appeal confirmed.

The powers of a Disciplinary Board

The Board may of course acquit the Member of the Charges against him.

If, however, there is an adverse finding, then the Board may adopt one or more of the following courses of action:

- a Caution;

- a Reprimand;

- a Severe Reprimand;

- the requirement for an undertaking;

- a fine of up to £5,000 in respect of each contravention – compared with the £1,000 maximum for a PCP;

- Conditional Continuing Membership;

- Suspension;

- Expulsion.

As with a PCP, the Disciplinary Board has power to order costs either way and has a discretion to order publication as set out above in relation to the PCP.

As distinct from a PCP, there are rights of appeal from a Disciplinary Board.

The Finding of the Disciplinary Board takes immediate effect unless the Board orders otherwise, so expulsion is not automatically stayed by the appeal process. However, the Member has the right of appeal against the finding of breach and/or the penalty imposed within a 21-day time limit. There is now a provision entitling the Chief Executive to appeal in cases where he considers that the penalty has been unduly lenient. Again there is a 21-day time limit. It is anticipated that this new power will be sparingly exercised.

Principles of sentencing adopted by the Disciplinary Board

Where a PCP has referred a case to a Disciplinary Board then it is usual for the Disciplinary Board to impose a penalty higher than any available to a PCP. However, in practice this may prove not to be the case due to perhaps more cogent mitigation being put forward.

The Disciplinary Board will consider the case entirely on its own merits and whilst it will take cognisance of the fact that a PCP may have referred a case on, due to perceived insufficiencies in its own powers, the Disciplinary Board will not be bound by such a conclusion.

(1) Expulsion

Unless there is strong mitigation, Members are at risk of being expelled for the following:

- dishonesty or lack of integrity;

- conviction for a serious criminal offence;

- serious breaches of the Accounts Rules;

- failure to co-operate with RICS and in particular deliberately misleading the Institution;

- gross incompetence or recklessness in relation to the conduct of professional activities;

- persistent failure to comply with the Rules in relation to Indemnity Insurance, Accounts and Lifelong Learning;

- serious non-compliance with Practice Statements;

- deliberate discrimination;

- breach of a required undertaking.

This list is not exhaustive. The range it covers, however, indicates the extreme importance to a Member of his case being properly put forward to the Board. A prudent Member will not only be present at the hearing, but will have instructed a suitable representative.

Regardless of the area of professional conduct in question, if a Member exhibits an unwillingness to be regulated by the Institution, then he is virtually certain to be expelled from it.

(2) Suspension

In practice, suspensions are quite rarely imposed. They may become even rarer since the availability of the sanction of Conditional Continuing Membership discussed below. Suspensions are often imposed in conjunction with other penalties and in cases where expulsion is considered by the Board to be too harsh, bearing in mind all the mitigating circumstances.

(3) Conditional Continuing Membership

This is a new power which is designed to be constructive and to lead to the cessation of the type of conduct that has brought the Member before the Disciplinary Board. This sanction has a regulatory as well as a disciplinary function.

(4) Fines

The same considerations apply as with PCPs.

(5) Publication

In practice, Members are often more aggrieved at the Order for publication of a penalty than they are at the penalty itself. This derives from the adverse business effects generated by the publicity.

PCP's, Disciplinary Boards and Appeal Boards all have the power to publish their Decisions through the mechanisms referred to above. The Rules imply an assumption that there will be publication unless a positive decision is taken otherwise.

It is felt that publication will be proper in the vast majority of cases. This is particularly so where proceedings are heard in private. There is now a general trend in the law towards transparency, and the public has a right to know not only which Members have offended, but what consequences have been provoked.

Such publication will be considered particularly important where the public may be at risk. If a surveyor has breached the Accounts Rules and caused the funds of his clients to be put at risk, then the public is entitled to know the facts before they entrust further funds to the surveyor in question.

Cases where publication may be considered inappropriate include those where there has been a substantial delay between the breach and the Finding, which delay was not the fault of the Member, and where no useful purpose would be served by publication.

(6) Costs

All three disciplinary bodies have the power to order costs either way.

The general principle is that costs follow the event, i.e. the loser pays.

At Disciplinary Board and Appeal Board levels, the claim for costs made by the Institution will include the costs of the Disciplinary Solicitor and a time limit will be imposed for payment.

In practice, a breakdown of the costs claim is supplied to the Member so that he may have the opportunity to make representations upon the claim being made against him. Where some of several Charges are not proved, then the Board may be expected to proceed on a pro rata basis.

The costs of Disciplinary Proceedings represent a burden upon the profession as a whole. Accordingly it is normally considered appropriate that the defaulting Member should bear the costs rather than the vast majority of Members who never offend at all.

Appeal Boards

Appeal Boards consider:

(1) appeals by Members aggrieved at the Decisions of Disciplinary Boards; and

(2) review of penalty at the behest of the Chief Executive.

The hearings take place in public.

An Appeal Board consists of between three and five members and will have at least the same number of members as the Disciplinary Board. The Chairman will be a Chartered Surveyor, and there will be at least one lay member. There is again a provision for a technical member where appropriate, and a Legal Assessor will be present.

No one who has heard the case at PCP or Disciplinary Board level will be eligible to sit on the Appeal Board.

In practice, a bundle of documents will be prepared by the Disciplinary Solicitor regardless of which party instigated the hearing.

The bundle will include all those documents before the Disciplinary Board, the Notice and Grounds of Appeal which have to be set out in writing and a Transcript of the Proceedings before the Disciplinary Board.

Appellant Members are entitled to attend with or without representation and are able to call up to two character witnesses with permission of the Board.

There are two possible procedures as follows:

(1) *Review*

Most Appeals proceed in this way. The Appeal Board is asked to review the decision of the Disciplinary Board and will do so in the light of the evidence and representations at Disciplinary Board level. The Grounds of Appeal will form the framework of the hearing and both parties are able to make representations as to how the Review should be resolved.

When proceeding in this way, an Appeal Board has a complete discretion but will give such consideration as it thinks appropriate to the decision of the Disciplinary Board.

(2) A *new hearing*

New hearings are far less frequent occurrences. They only take place if the Appellant seeks a new hearing and if the Appeal Board in its discretion considers it necessary. It is most unlikely that permission would be given for a new hearing where the Appeal was against the penalty and not the finding of the Disciplinary Board.

In either event, a documentary procedure which has been disclosed to the Member will be followed, and the result of the proceedings may be expected there and then.

Members considering appealing should carefully note that in the event of an unsuccessful appeal, the Board may impose a sentence more severe than that imposed by the

Disciplinary Board. In practice, this rarely occurs, but the attention of the Member is specifically drawn to this point when he is informed of his rights of appeal.

Again, the Appeal Board has powers with respect to costs and publication.

All decisions of Appeal Boards take immediate effect and there is no further appeal within the Institution.

The Chief Executive

Certain powers are delegated to the Chief Executive and they are exercised after an Investigation has taken place. The powers are limited in range with £300 being the maximum fine per complaint or allegation. These powers only apply in cases of first offenders and if the Member is aggrieved at the exercise of the power, then he has 21 days in which to say so and the matter is referred on to a PCP or Disciplinary Board.

The precise ambit of the Chief Executive's discretion is clearly set out in an Appendix to the Institution's Disciplinary Rules which are available to all Members.

Other individual matters

The consequences of Expulsion

Once such an Order takes effect, the name of the Member is removed from the Register and he ceases for all purposes to be a Member of the Institution. His Diplomas of Membership are immediately returnable and he will not be entitled to use any designation or description which implies membership or former membership of the Institution.

The consequences of Suspension

Again Diplomas are immediately returnable.

During the period of suspension, the Member cannot exercise any of the rights or privileges of membership, nor use any designation or description as in the case of an expelled Member.

However, there is a very important distinction in that suspended Members remain in all other respects subject to the provisions of the Bye-Laws and Rules of Conduct. They can be disciplined for breaches occurring during the period of suspension.

Therefore, in particular, the suspended Member must comply with the Regulations in relation to Accounts and Professional Indemnity Insurance, notwithstanding his suspended status.

Furthermore, a suspended Member is under a duty to forthwith notify all his existing clients of the fact his suspension in writing at the first available opportunity.

Therefore the position of a suspended Member is a difficult one indeed. Whilst suspended he has all the obligations, but none of the privileges of membership and informing all his clients of his suspended status can have disastrous effects upon his practice.

The burden of proof

Generally speaking decisions are made on the 'balance of probabilities', i.e. is the breach more likely than not to have been committed?

However, in particularly serious cases involving dishonesty, the 'beyond reasonable doubt' approach of the Criminal Courts may be preferred.

The more serious the allegation, the higher the test. At Disciplinary Board and Appeal Board level, the Legal Assessor will advise.

Resignation

It is by no means unusual for Members subject to the disciplinary process to tender their resignation to the Institution as a purported means of avoiding the Proceedings.

However, efforts to do so are frustrated by operation of Bye-Law 22(4), which provides that once a Member has been notified that a complaint or allegation has been made against him, or that a conviction, bankruptcy or certain other matters have been notified to the Institution, he shall not be entitled to resign until all Proceedings have been concluded, and those Proceedings may be continued despite the attempted resignation.

If, however, a resignation has been tendered in writing, and accepted in writing, by the Institution, then there will no longer be any jurisdiction to proceed with the matter.

Reinstatement

The fact that a Member has been expelled from the membership does not of itself mean that he can never regain his professional status.

Bye-Law 12 allows for reinstatement either
unconditionally or upon such terms as may be ordered.
The onus is on the expelled Member to make an
application in writing for reinstatement.

Effective submissions to PCPs or Boards

If a Member finds himself subject to any of these
processes, then it is essential that his submissions are
properly targeted for maximum effect. The Panel or
Board dealing with the matter will be particularly
interested in the following.

(1) The nature and seriousness of the breach including
     whether it involved dishonesty, or recklessness.

(2) The risk of loss or damage to the public.

(3) The previous record – particularly any
     contraventions in the relatively recent past.

(4) The length of time over which the breach occurred
     and whether it involved systemic failings.

(5) The number of breaches.

(6) The attitude of the Member towards compliance.
     Note that specific credit will be given if the Member
     himself drew the breach to the attention of the
     Institution. Other relevant matters here are remedial
     steps and contrition.

(7) Any benefit obtained from the breach.

(8) Any compensatory steps taken.

(9) The degree of co-operation with the Institution.

(10) The financial position of the Member.

In considering these aspects, the Member should be aware that the PCP or Board will have in mind:

- previous decisions in similar cases;

- the need for deterrence; and

- the need to demonstrate that firm action is taken in the public interest.

Accordingly any Member in professional Disciplinary Proceedings should ensure that he addresses the PCP or Board with the above in mind.

Whatever has happened in the past, it is essential that the Member adopts a very responsible attitude towards the Disciplinary Proceedings. When mitigating, by far the best word that can be used is 'sorry', and there should be a recognition that professional misbehaviour not only impacts upon the Member, but also upon the whole of the profession.

The Member in difficulties should also liaise with the Disciplinary Solicitor who will be pleased to advise with regard to practical steps that the Respondent can take, for instance with regard to representation. The Disciplinary Solicitor will not of course be in a position to advise on the merits of the case.

The atmosphere at all hearings is as informal as can properly be the case. The Chairman and (before the Boards) the Legal Assessor will do their utmost to ensure that the Member represents himself as effectively as possible. In particular, they will explain that if he chooses to give evidence rather than make a statement, then more weight will be attached to the Member's submissions.

Giving evidence, however, will expose the Member to cross-examination.

Boards will wish to be assured that the conduct in question will not be repeated, but in imposing sentence, the paramount considerations will be the reputation of the profession and the maintenance of public confidence.

Prompt communication by the Member of his position in the Proceedings will serve to reduce the costs that he is likely to be ordered to pay. This is yet another example of the pro-active approach that should be adopted.

Accounts

Before turning to specific provisions which impose obligations upon Members with respect to their handling of their clients' money, consideration will be given to the general principles which apply.

Many Chartered Surveyors will receive clients' funds as part of their day-to-day practice. The essential point is that those funds are not given to the Member; rather they are entrusted to him. The Member holds the funds as a trustee for the party or parties ultimately entitled to them

These monies are not the funds of the Member and they must at all times be kept separately from the Member's own funds.

The profession of Chartered Surveyor depends upon honourable conduct by the Members for the maintenance of its reputation, and this is thrown into sharp focus when the handling of clients' funds comes to be considered.

It goes without saying that Members must be punctilious in their handling of clients' funds. Client account is sacrosanct. A Member must never have recourse to clients' money for his own purposes and neither must he use the funds of one client for the purposes of another. No client's ledger must ever show a debit balance.

Whilst the Rules of Conduct provide detailed obligations, the fundamental duty to account honestly for clients' money must be the paramount consideration for every Member.

Bye-Law 19(7)

Bye-Law 19(7) sets out the general framework for the more detailed Regulations. It imposes a threefold obligation as follows.

(1) To maintain a client account or accounts separate from the Member's (or his company's) own bank account.

(2) To account properly for all monies received and paid on behalf of any person entitled to such an account.

(3) To maintain client account records in accordance with the Regulations.

Accordingly, this stresses the fundamental obligation to keep the funds belonging to clients separate from those belonging to the Member. Proper accounting records will establish that this duty has been discharged.

The Rules of Conduct

Conduct Rules 28–34 apply.

Rule 28 gives the Governing Council the power to make rules, which are found in Part III of Schedule 1 to Conduct Regulation 27.1.

These general Rules of Conduct provide for the following.

(1) The obligation to separate funds so that clients' money may be available on demand – Rule 30.

(2) An obligation to maintain properly written accounts so as to enable the current balance held on behalf of each client to be identified – Rule 31.

(3) An obligation to deliver to the Institution once in every period of 12 months, a Certificate signed by the Member as to whether or not he has held clients' funds in that period – Rule 32.

(4) The power vested in the Institution to inspect the accounts of a Member – Rule 33.

(5) The power of the Governing Council to waive or modify any accounts provisions in a particular case – Rule 34.

The detailed provisions

These are found in the Schedule referred to above. Helpful definitions are set out of which the following are particularly important.

'CLIENT'

This includes past, present and prospective clients and means:

(a) any person or body for whom the Member or his firm is acting in any capacity;

(b) any other person or body on whose behalf the Members holds or receive clients' money;

(c)   in Scotland the general body of proprietors of units in a tenement property.

'CLIENT ACCOUNT'

This means a current or deposit account at a bank or building society into which clients' money is paid.

'CLIENTS' MONEY'

This means any money received or held by a Member or his firm which does not belong solely to him, his firm or a connected person and over which there is exclusive control.

'CONNECTED PERSON'

This means in relation to a Member, his partner or a director of his firm.

It should also be noted that 'exclusive control' means that control of clients' money is restricted to a Member, a connected person and an employee of his firm. The term 'firm' includes a sole principal, a partnership, a limited liability partnership or a company incorporated with limited or unlimited liability offering surveying services.

The scope of the Rules

The Rules discussed below apply to a Member who is practising as a surveyor or is held out to the public to be practising as a surveyor, and who is either:

(a)   a sole principal of; or

(b)   a partner in; or

(c)   a director of

a firm offering surveying services.

The obligation to maintain a client account

Rule 16 of the Schedule provides that it is mandatory for a Member receiving or holding clients' money to keep at least one client account.

Members opening a client account must be careful to ensure that it is properly named. The title of the account must include the word 'client', the name of the Member's firm and the full name of the client if the account is a discrete client account, i.e. a client account into which funds are paid belonging exclusively to one client.

Rule 17 imposes requirements upon a Member when opening a client account. Before so doing it is the responsibility of the Member to ensure that the bank or building society at which the account is maintained has agreed in writing that:

(1) all money standing to the credit of that account is clients' money;

(2) the bank or building society is not entitled to combine the account with any other or exercise any set off in relation to the funds in that account;

(3) any interest earned on the account shall be credited to the account save where the Member has obtained the written agreement of his client for the interest to be retained by the practice;

(4) any charges in relation to the account must not be debited to it unless it is a discrete client account and the Member has written instructions from the client.

These basic rules in relation to the setting up of client accounts are particularly important. Should they not be followed and a Member dies, or a receiver or liquidator is appointed with respect to his affairs or the affairs of his firm, then unless the Rules have been complied with, it will be very difficult and sometimes impossible to establish, that the funds in the account in question belong to third parties, rather than to the surveyor.

It is compulsory under Rule 16 for Members to notify their clients of the identity of the account in which their money is held. The surveyor has by necessary implication chosen the account in question and clients may wish to suggest that a more advantageous account in terms of interest should be utilised. It is, however, understood that Members will wish to keep their client account book-keeping as simple as possible, and a multiplicity of client accounts should be avoided where possible.

Payments into and out of client accounts

Rule 19 imposes the basic obligation upon a surveyor to pay clients' funds into a client account within three working days of receipt.

This provision does not simply apply to clients' money as defined above, but also to a cheque or bank draft which includes clients' funds as well as the Members' own funds. Further, it applies to funds introduced by the surveyor to replace money withdrawn in contravention of the Rules.

Essentially, therefore, any breaches of the Rules must be rectified immediately. A failure to do so will invite severe disciplinary sanction.

However, money received as payment in advance for work yet to be undertaken or completed need not be paid into a client account as long as the Member has notified the client in writing that the RICS Clients' Money Protection Scheme will not apply and the client consents in writing to his money being withheld from a client account.

It is, however, simpler and indeed preferable for such funds to be paid into a client account for the avoidance of any misunderstanding.

Rule 21 deals with payments from a client account.

Essentially money cannot be withdrawn for or on behalf of a client which exceeds the money held. This reflects the basic principle that no client ledger must ever show a debit balance.

Money can only be withdrawn from a client account if it is properly required either for or on behalf of a client, or to reimburse the Member for money expended on behalf of a client, e.g. proper fees or disbursements.

There is a converse provision relating to breaches caused by money other than clients' funds being paid into client accounts. Those funds must be withdrawn within three working days of awareness. It is just as much of a breach to have excessive funds in the client account as it is for there to be insufficient funds in the account. In such circumstances, it will be likely that there has been a mixing of funds.

Where withdrawals from client account relate to the Member reimbursing himself for money paid on behalf of a client or to taking fees and disbursements, then the withdrawal can only take place if:

(a) it has been authorised in writing by the client in advance;

or

(b) an invoice or other written notice for such payment has been delivered to the client and no objection is made within a reasonable time to the withdrawal taking place.

The term 'reasonable time' is not defined. In construing the term, it may be thought that a client, who has been properly informed of the withdrawal and objects to it, may be expected to make his views known quite promptly!

Discrete client accounts

Where a client instructs the Member to pay funds into such an account, then the Member must comply. Thereafter only funds held on behalf of the client in question can be paid into that account.

As distinct from the prohibition applying to the general client bank account, a Member is permitted to operate an arrangement for the regular direct debiting of monies from such an account.

Generally speaking, funds cannot be debited to such an account in excess of the balance held, but there are minor exceptions set out in Rule 23.

Transfer between client accounts

The general principle here is that a Member can only transfer funds from the ledger account of one client to that of another client in circumstances in which the transfer would have been permitted as a payment out of the first account. Rule 24 applies.

Who can operate a client account?

There are specific provisions in Rule 25 as to which parties are entitled to pay money into or out of client accounts.

The only persons who can be properly mandated are:

(a) a Member; or

(b) a partner or a co-director of a Member of the same limited liability partnership as a Member; or

(c) a Member of the Institution employed under a Contract of Service by a Member or his firm; or

(d) an accountant employed by a Member under a Contract of Service and who is a member of a recognised supervisory body; or

(e) any other person who is authorised in writing by the Institution.

Furthermore, any mandated signatory other than a Member must at all times be the subject of a fidelity guarantee in the Member's professional indemnity insurance policy.

Again, this is a very important Rule which is frequently overlooked. It is the Member who is responsible as trustee, as well as under the terms of the Rules, for his clients' funds and it is essential that only those properly mandated operate the client account. Should for instance the Member seek the permission of the Institution to have a member of staff, e.g. a book-keeper, mandated to operate a client account, then a very careful approach will be adopted before any approval is given.

The obligation to keep proper records

Members must not only be punctilious in their handling of clients' funds, they must be able to demonstrate that characteristic.

Rule 26 provides for the obligation to maintain at all times properly written up books of account to show a Member's dealings with all funds dealt with through the client account with the records reflecting these dealings separately in relation to each client. A current balance held on behalf of each client must always be shown.

When a Member deals with clients' funds, then a record must be made either in a clients' cash book or in a record of ledger transfers, and also in a clients' ledger.

Experience shows that when this Rule is breached, then other substantive breaches are likely to follow, e.g. improper withdrawals from the client account.

It is recommended that the book-keeping of a practice should be carried out daily, or in the case of a very small practice, weekly at the least. Proper and up-to-date book-keeping is the best mechanism to avoid other problems.

There is also an obligation to carry out client account bank reconciliations at least once in every calendar month.

The balance on the client's cash book must be reconciled with:

- the balance in the client account shown on the bank statement; and

- the total of each client's balance in the clients' ledger.

This reconciliation must be carried out and a statement of it maintained within the books of account. No more than five weeks must pass between one reconciliation and the next.

If, however, the client account has not been used since the last reconciliation, then the calendar-monthly obligation does not apply. However, as a matter of good practice, it is suggested that it should be carried out – it will hardly be an onerous task in those circumstances.

Members must maintain a list of all persons for whom they have been holding money and a list of banks and building societies in which money has been held.

All the book-keeping records must be preserved for at least six years from the date of the last entry in the account. They must be made available not only for the Member's own accountant, but also if appropriate to an Investigating Accountant appointed by the Institution.

The bank reconciliation is another vital mechanism. It will bring to the attention of the Member any breaches that may have unwittingly taken place, whereupon the obligation to restore funds within three working days is triggered. Balanced reconciliations will demonstrate compliance with the Rules.

In the chapter on Conduct Unbefitting, comment was made as to the obligations of a Member to report misconduct. Rule 27 of the Schedule provides a specific example of such an obligation existing. A Member must notify the Institution immediately of any deliberate misappropriation of clients' money immediately that he becomes aware of it, and he must replace it from his own or his firm's resources. It is suggested that this must apply to circumstances where it is the Member who has been guilty of the misappropriation. Where this has taken place, the Member will be in very serious difficulties indeed, but will at least gain some credit by complying with his duty to report and restore.

Certificates and Accountant's Reports

Reference has been made above to the obligation upon a Member to deliver an annual Certificate in relation to clients' funds which the Member signs himself.

If the Member has held clients' funds, then additionally he is responsible for the annual delivery of an Accountant's Report to the Institution. This is due within six months of the end of the relevant accounting period, and as with the Certificate must be delivered once in every 12 months.

Where a Member has two or more places of business, he may adopt separate accounting periods for each place of business.

Failure to comply with these provisions is likely to lead to disciplinary action. Furthermore, pursuant to Bye-Law 22B there is a provision for imposition of fines in default of delivery of the Certificate, and (where appropriate) the Accountant's Report. In these circumstances, Rule 41 provides that where there has been a failure to deliver the documents within 28 days of the due date, then the Chief Executive may, by notice in writing, demand fines as follows:

(a) first four weeks following expiry of the notice that a fine will become payable if the required actions have not been taken until the actions are fulfilled – a maximum of £30 per week or part thereof;

(b) next four weeks – a maximum of £50 per week or part thereof;

(c) subsequent weeks – £100 per four weeks.

These fines are payable within a period which must be notified to the Member and will be not less than 28 days from the notice.

Once this procedure has been followed, if the Member either fails without reasonable excuse to furnish the material required within the specified period, or alternatively asks the Chief Executive within 28 days from the Notice to refer the matter to a Disciplinary Board, then the Chief Executive is under a duty to refer the matter to a Disciplinary Board.

Members must remember that whilst in practice the Accountant's Report is prepared by an accountant, the responsibility for delivering the Report remains with the Member. Inaction by the accountant will not excuse a breach.

Accounts inspections

Rule 30 gives the Chief Executive the power to require an inspection of a Member's accounts.

This power can either be exercised on a random basis or specifically as a reaction to information being obtained by the Institution which leads to the conclusion that there may be accounts problems.

The Member will receive written notification of the inspection and his duties to produce accounting documents for inspection will be made clear.

The Investigating Accountant may either be employed by the Institution or be a Chartered Accountant in private practice. A written Report will be produced upon the inspection, disclosed to the member and may form the basis of disciplinary action.

If the result of such an inspection is that the Member has breached the Rules in relation to accounts, then a Professional Conduct Panel or Disciplinary Board or Appeals Board can in its discretion order a payment towards the costs of this inspection.

There are specific Rules regulating Accountant's Reports from the points of view of:

(1) the qualifications of the reporting accountant;

(2) the form of the Report; and

(3) the scope of the work to be carried out by the accountant.

Rule 22 allows auctioneers, subject to conditions, to pay office money into client account. Livestock auctioneers may, subject to conditions, be exempt from the Rules (except Rules 28–31) in connection with livestock auctions.

There is no substitute for a full reading of the relevant Rules which form a vital part of the bedrock of self-regulation of the profession.

Disciplinary action

Breaches of the Rules in relation to accounts are highly likely to result in Disciplinary Proceedings and the most serious breaches will certainly be dealt with by a Disciplinary Board.

Should dishonesty be found, then expulsion is virtually inevitable.

Furthermore, where the breaches are serious although not dishonest, the Member is at risk of expulsion unless there are strong mitigating circumstances.

The protection of the public will be the paramount consideration on sentence and the question of loss or risk of loss is an important factor.

Self-preservation

The importance of compliance with these provisions cannot be over-emphasised. Proper conduct with respect to the funds of others goes to the very heart of the professional relationship and the trustee status of the Member.

Compliance with these provisions depends on administrative and managerial expertise. Professionals often complain that this is not their forte. That is readily understood by the Institution, but responsibility cannot be delegated.

The following points are intended as helpful suggestions.

- Start off on the right foot. Open your client accounts with reputable institutions, obtain the appropriate documentary confirmations when the accounts are open and bear careful attention to their titles.

- Scrutinise bank statements carefully. Ensure that no improper charges or interest are debited to your client accounts.

- Be efficient with the banking. Ensure that you make your payments into client account within three working days but preferably on the day of receipt. Make a note of the ledger to be credited, not only on vouchers such as paying in slips for the Accounts Department but also on the paying in slips themselves.

- Be absolutely sure to devote appropriate resources to your Accounts Department. Employ a suitable number of staff and be careful to take up proper references in advance. Whilst administrative overheads can be high, they will pale into insignificance when set against the consequences of non-compliance with the appropriate Rules. Professional survival depends upon proper book-keeping.

- Never carry out your own book-keeping unless you are totally confident in your own ability. If the experience of the solicitors' profession is anything to go by, then it will be rare indeed for a Member to be able to carry on his own practice and keep his own books without imposing an almost impossible burden upon himself.

- Supervise accounts staff properly. Show a keen interest in the affairs of the Accounts Department and have a thorough grasp of the work being done there. Make sure that you see and check all bank reconciliations and counter-sign them.

- Breaches can occur in even the best ordered of organisations. Be sure that these come to your immediate attention and that they are rectified immediately. Never cover your tracks.

- Be certain to comply when clients ask for an account of the monies held on their behalf. Communicate promptly and set out the situation clearly. Even if you consider that a request for an account is unnecessary, you must still comply with your duty.

- Make sure that your accountants commence their auditing work for your annual Accountants Report as soon as possible after the end of the accounting period. Remember that the responsibility for the delivery of the Report is yours and the six months allowed can soon slip by.

- Particularly in the early days of a new practice, it is sensible to ask the accountants to carry out their audit in two separate stages – the first being six months or so into the year. This spreads the cost of accountancy fees and gives you an early and clear picture of how you are doing. The accountant will in any event have to reconcile your client account at two separate dates during the year.

- Ensure that you have adequate IT support. Always maintain a back-up set of accounts and have help on hand should anything go wrong with the technology. That having been said there is of course no objection to manual accounts being kept, although these days they are increasingly rare.

- Always seek help in times of difficulty. Your first port of call should be your own accountant, but remember that the Institution will also be able to give guidance. When that is sought remember to disclose the full facts so that an informed opinion can be taken.

Finally, remember that as with so many other conduct provisions, an honest honourable and transparent approach will effectively avoid difficulties. The Accounts Department can be considered the engine room of the practice and its smooth running will facilitate a successful passage through professional life.

Financial responsibilities

It is a sad fact of business life that some Members will face financial difficulties which can lead to their insolvency and possible bankruptcy. Somewhat unusually amongst professions, the Institution has a specific Bye-Law relating to financial failure and relating it to a conduct offence.

Bye-Law 19(9) applies to Members practising on their own account, in partnership, as a director of a company or a member of a limited liability partnership.

There are three distinct provisions and each will be examined individually.

Bye-Law 19(9)(a) provides that every Member shall promptly discharge his business and personal debts fully as and when they fall due.

It is important to note that the provision does not merely relate to the affairs of the Member's practice, but also to the financial conduct of the Member's personal affairs.

As will be seen, the approach to conduct offences arising from financial failures has changed over the years. When the Bye-Laws and associated Rules of Conduct were first established, all Members of the Institution in private practice traded either on their own account or in partnership. It was then considered that financial failure culminating in a bankruptcy (see below) would involve a distinct likelihood of suspension or expulsion.

The rationale behind this provision is that members of the public are entitled to expect professional people not only to possess sufficient technical expertise, but also to exhibit prudence and responsibility in the conduct of their own affairs as distinct from their ability to represent others.

Other professions deal with this type of situation differently. For instance, in the solicitors' profession there is a scheme of issuing Practising Certificates which can be suspended, withdrawn or rendered conditional in certain circumstances. The Institution does not have such a scheme and accordingly there is no regulatory halfway house. Insolvency is a conduct offence.

The fact that the Institution has made such a provision underlines the gravity with which such failure will be regarded.

A breach of this provision does not require the existence of a Judgment against the Member. Neither is it a defence for a Member to assert that he had sufficient financial resources to pay the debt at the time, i.e. that he was not insolvent. It is the failure to pay the debt that triggers the breach.

Bye-Law 19(9)(b) provides that every Member shall so conduct his business and personal financial affairs to as to ensure that he is not adjudicated bankrupt, or have proceedings which are analogous to bankruptcy instituted against him anywhere in the world, and/or does not enter into an arrangement or composition with or for the benefit of his creditors.

The existence of this provision does not in any way restrict the terms of Bye-Law 19(9)(a). It is, however, expressed in more specific terms than the preceding provision. Again the Bye-Law relates not only to the Member's practice, but also his private financial affairs. The following points should be noted.

- A Bankruptcy Order amounts to a breach.

- In the case of analogous proceedings, it is the issue rather than the conclusion of the proceedings which will create an offence.

- The financial failure need not arise in our jurisdiction.

- Whilst entering into an Individual Voluntary Arrangement ('IVA') with creditors may be a responsible and prudent step to take, it still amounts to a conduct offence.

Bye-Law 19(9)(c) provides that where a Member is a director of a company or is a Member of a limited liability partnership in either case offering surveying services to the public, then he shall ensure that the company or partnership promptly discharges its debts as and when they fall due, and is not subject to the appointment of an office-holder for the purpose of insolvency proceedings under the *Insolvency Act* 1986 or any analogous provisions in any jurisdiction.

This is a specific provision relating to practice in a company or partnership context and provides a similar obligation to achieve solvency as applies to those members practising in other ways.

Again, there is no requirement for a Judgment against the company or partnership and it will be no defence to establish that the debt could have been paid but was not paid. Once more the relevant financial failure does not have to arise in this jurisdiction.

From the above it can be seen that very strict requirements are imposed by this Bye-Law. How are breaches perceived and dealt with by the Institution?

The characteristics of an Individual Voluntary Arrangement

The Institution is acutely aware that those Members experiencing financial difficulties will be anxious to resolve them at the earliest possible moment.

In some cases, Members are advised that their difficulties can best be dealt with by entering into an IVA and the Institution would never wish to inhibit such a course of action where it is based on proper financial advice.

An IVA is an alternative to bankruptcy which is quite reasonably often regarded as the last resort. The IVA is a less formal procedure than bankruptcy and is open to those who are already subject to bankruptcy proceedings. The procedure is extremely flexible varying from case to case. Essentially, the debtor makes a payment proposal (i.e. one other than one hundred pence in the pound when payment is due) explaining why it is more advantageous than bankruptcy or a continuation of it: It can, for instance, be based on assets that would not be available in a bankruptcy (e.g. donated by a third party) or earnings that would not otherwise be possible.

The proposal for an IVA is prepared by the debtor himself assisted by a Licensed Insolvency Practitioner. The proposal commences with a statement from the debtor that he is unable to pay his debts as and when they fall due so an IVA may be a means to avoid bankruptcy but the proposal is a prima facie breach of Bye-Law 19(9)(a).

Initially an application is made to a Court which has the power to stay all other legal proceedings. In particular no Bankruptcy Petition can be heard during the period provided for by the Court.

A report is prepared by a nominee who must be a Licensed Insolvency Practitioner. If the report is positive then a Creditors Meeting will take place after the report is published. All creditors are shown the proposal, a statement of the debtor's affairs and the report of the nominee.

To enable the IVA to go forward the debtor must have the agreement of over 75 per cent in value of the creditors who vote on it at a Creditors Meeting.

If approval is obtained then a supervisor (again essentially a Licensed Insolvency Practitioner) is appointed. He will report to the Court and implement the proposal that has been approved. Insolvency legislation from 1996 has recently been amended by the *Enterprise Act* 2002. This received Royal Assent on 7 November 2002. Changes to corporate insolvency and the powers of trustees in bankruptcy were effective from 15 September 2003 and other individual insolvency provisions came into force on 1 April 2004. One of these is the facility of a fast-track IVA procedure under which the Official Receiver can be nominee and supervisor. (The Official Receiver is a civil servant who exercises his functions under the general directions of the Secretary of State for Trade and Industry and is an officer of Courts with insolvency jurisdiction). The reason a bankrupt may try to get an IVA approved is that it is a ground upon which a Court may annul a Bankruptcy Order. The effect of annulment is that the Order has never been made.

Publicity is limited and the costs can be lower than those incurred in a bankruptcy.

The IVA however cannot affect the rights of creditors who have the benefit of security unless they expressly agree to the arrangement.

Creditors receive distributions throughout the period covered by the IVA, but if the debtor breaches the terms agreed by the creditors, then almost inevitably bankruptcy will result.

Bankruptcy

An individual may be made bankrupt upon a petition to a Court presented by his creditor(s), the supervisor of a failed IVA or the individual himself.

The Court will make a Bankruptcy Order if it is satisfied that the debtor cannot pay his debts.

It is then usual for the Official Receiver to be appointed receiver and manager of the estate of the bankrupt. The

Official Receiver carries out an investigation into the reason for the financial failure where he thinks it is necessary and prepares a report for the creditors.

A Creditors Meeting is called if there are significant assets with a view to possibly appointing a Licensed Insolvency Practitioner to be trustee of the bankrupt's estate. If not the Official Receiver will adopt this function.

There is extra publicity. A Bankruptcy Order is advertised in the *London Gazette* and Creditors Meetings are also advertised in local press.

The Trustee is responsible for realising the assets of the bankrupt and distributing them amongst creditors in order of priority. Secured creditors have first claim.

Whilst the bankrupt has a right to the basic requirements of daily life and employment, he loses all other rights to his property. Assets received between the Bankruptcy Order and discharge from proceedings, including inheritances, may be claimed for the estate in bankruptcy.

A bankrupt will not be prevented from earning his living but needs the consent of the Court if he wishes to act as a company director or even be involved in the management of the company. His ability to obtain credit is limited.

From 1 April 2004, bankrupts who have failed through no fault of their own and who co-operate with the Official Receiver will be discharged from bankruptcy after a maximum of 12 months. This means they will have no further legal liability to pay debts that were part of the bankruptcy (some debts such as criminal fines and student loans survive bankruptcy) and restrictions will cease to apply to them. There is, however, a new Bankruptcy Restriction Order regime to tackle those who have abused the trust of their creditors to the detriment of the public at large under which restrictions may apply for between two and fifteen years. These periods mirror the minimum and maximum periods of disqualification possible under the *Company Directors' Disqualification Act* 1996 for company directors, who are not personally bankrupt, found to be unfit to act as such.

The approach of the Institution

It has already been noted that hitherto suspension or expulsion was felt to be an almost certain result of financial failure. Times, however, have changed.

The first priority for a Member in financial difficulties which amount to a breach of Bye-Law 19(9) in any of its aspects is to keep the Institution fully informed of the position at all times. Even where the news is bad, the Institution has a right to know all the facts relating to the Member in breach.

It will be powerful mitigation in any disciplinary proceedings for the Member to establish that he has been frank and open with the Institution throughout.

The Institution accepts that the ability to practise under limited liability coupled with periodic recessions has resulted in business failure becoming perhaps more common than hitherto. It is understood that financial failure may well be self-inflicted, but on the other hand it may not. Circumstances entirely outside the control of the Member may come into play.

Indeed, a Disciplinary Board may even conclude that a financial failure would not be a breach of the Bye-Law if there were exceptional or compelling circumstances existing in the particular case. It should be assumed however that such cases will be very few and far between, and accordingly financial failures within the scope of the Bye-Law will amount to conduct offences.

The degree of personal blameworthiness is a crucial factor for both the Institution in the conduct of its inquiry and the Disciplinary Board in its decision as to penalty. Relevant questions therefore include the following.

- Could the failure have been foreseen or avoided?

- What remedial action could have been taken and might it have prevented the failure?

- What measure of control did the Member have over the affairs of the practice?

- What subsequent steps has the Member taken to mitigate the effect of the financial failure on his creditors?

- What steps has the Member taken to avoid a recurrence of such failure?

- What publicity has surrounded the financial failure?

- How were the interests of clients protected?

- How were the interests of employees protected?

- What was the financial effect on the shareholders and what actions did they take to mitigate the failure?

The answers to these questions enable a view to be taken as to whether the Member has behaved with acceptable responsibility or otherwise.

It is usual for the above specific questions to be put to a Member by the Institution in correspondence arising out of a financial failure. Each question should be carefully answered and supporting documentation supplied.

Members should be aware that in the absence of extenuating circumstances a Disciplinary Board is likely to make an Order for Expulsion in a case of gross incompetence or recklessness in relation to the conduct or management of the Member's professional activities. It may be the case that professional financial failure will he looked upon more severely than will personal failure, but no specific principle to this effect has been enunciated.

Self-preservation

The fact that the Financial Failure Bye-Law is unusual amongst professionals brings home the seriousness with which it is regarded by the Institution.

The following suggestions may be of some help.

(1) Professional people are trained so as to acquire the appropriate technical expertise. They are not trained as business managers.

It is therefore essential for a Member to obtain his own business expertise and to devote sufficient financial resources to the proper running of the practice. This is distinct from the devotion of appropriate resources to the Accounts Department (see separate chapter – Accounts) but relates to the ensuring of business viability.

Also seek outside assistance, i.e. from your Accountants and, if thought absolutely necessary, Management Consultants.

(2) Keep a very careful eye on cash flow. Read the practice bank statements yourself immediately they come in and have a proper system of credit control. Surveyors are not banks and should not allow their clients to treat them as such.

(3) Have a reference to payment of fees in your Terms of Engagement. Keep the client informed with regard to fees. Bills that come as a shock are much less likely to be promptly paid.

(4) Do not only impose proper financial disciplines upon yourself – ensure that they also apply to your staff. The responsibility, however, is yours and proper supervision of staff both technically and financially should always be in place.

(5) Seek immediate legal advice upon any financial claims against you that you consider to be unjustified. Never bury your head in the sand and allow Judgments to be entered against you by default.

(6) Where difficulties arise that cannot be surmounted and you find yourself in breach, then it is essential that you advise the Institution. Remember that it is almost inevitable that financial failure will come to the attention of the Institution and you will receive a great deal of credit from having communicated the news yourself. Failure to keep the Institution advised of such problems may also amount to conduct unbefitting a Chartered Surveyor which would only add to the professional difficulties that flow from such failure.

(7) Remember that personal financial failure is just as much a breach as is business failure. It is dealt with in the same way by the Institution and should be approached in the same way by the Member. The Institution is not insensitive and will give a Member due credit for a pro-active approach to this aspect of professional conduct as with any other.

Relations with the Institution

The general duty

The Institution is charged with the heavy burden of maintaining the reputation of the profession as being an honourable one. Also it seeks to promote the interests of Members in many ways, not the least of which is the stress that is placed upon the professional status of Members which provides a commercial advantage.

As befits its status, the profession regulates itself and its ability to do so effectively is crucial to the maintenance of public confidence.

Any system of this type operates by consent. Self-regulation is these days regarded as a privilege rather than a right, and for the privilege to be retained it is essential that the Institution is able to demonstrate that the system is effective.

It is a fundamental principle of professional conduct that Members must at all times co-operate with their professional body in the discharge of its functions.

In most instances there is no problem. The vast majority of Members do co-operate, but the small minority that does not causes inordinate difficulty and expense.

Regulating the profession brings with it a very heavy administrative burden and those who fail to co-operate as required will face disciplinary sanctions.

This has been touched upon in the separate chapter on Conduct Unbefitting which reflects the general duty of co-operation that is imposed upon all Members. The other side of this coin is that the Institution will freely give advice and assistance to Members seeking guidance in the face of professional difficulties.

A serious case of non-co-operation will be characterised as conduct unbefitting, but in addition to this general duty, there are specific instances in which the Rules lay down a particular obligation.

Specific duties

(1) Particulars of practice

Conduct Rule 13 provides that a Member shall, within 28 days of being required to do so, provide to the Institution such particulars as are required:

(a) of his firm if he is carrying on professional practice as a sole principal partner or director of the firm; or

(b) of his employment if he is employed under a contract of service or a contract for services.

Furthermore, where a Member has provided such particulars and any changes of circumstances occur with respect to the notified particulars, then there is an obligation to provide full particulars of the change within 28 days after the change has come into effect.

The purpose of this Rule is to enable the Institution to know where its Members are and what they are doing.

Also the information provided enables the Institution to make a judgement as to whether particular Members are subject to, for instance, the Accounts Rules and to assess proper compliance with, for instance, the Professional Indemnity Insurance Rules.

A breach of this Rule is triggered by the Institution making a request for particulars and those particulars either not being forthcoming, or not being updated in the case of change.

However, prudent Members seeking to set up in practice for the first time will no doubt seek guidance from the Institution. A pack of documents will be issued to the Member and will no doubt provide considerable assistance.

In issuing this documentation, the Institution will request that the Member completes a Private Practice Questionnaire which will involve details being given not only of the Member completing this document, but also details of any partners or co-directors.

(2) Conduct inquiries

Rule 14 provides that a Member shall co-operate with staff and any appointees of the Institution who:

(a) are investigating a complaint or allegation made against a Member or a Member's firm; or

(b) have sent to the Member a written enquiry relating to the Member's

(i) compliance with the Bye-Laws, any Rules or undertaking which may be given to the Institution, or

(ii) conviction of an offence involving embezzlement, theft, corruption, fraud or dishonesty of any kind or any other offence carrying on first conviction the possibility of a custodial sentence; or

(c) are undertaking a visit of inspection and shall provide full and prompt expenses to their inquiries.

Points to note are as follows.

(1) The obligation not only applies to a situation where there has been a complaint by a client or member of the public, but also where the Institution is making an allegation against the Member.

(2) The Rule also applies where there is no allegation but merely an inquiry by the Institution with a view to establishing whether or not a Member has beached any conduct provision.

(3) The duty to co-operate is not only owed to the Institution but also to its appointees, for instance an Investigating Accountant instructed by the Institution to carry out a spot check.

(4) There is no time limit set out in the Rule. The Member's reply must be 'full and prompt'. Generally speaking it will be a breach if there is failure to comply with a reasonable time limit set out by the Institution in the letter in question.

The Rule is drafted widely and it would be dangerous for a Member to seek to find a loophole so as to provide a defence to an allegation of breach of this Regulation.

Members must assume that when a question is asked of them by the Institution, then they have an obligation to answer.

(3) Lifelong Learning

The separate chapter on this subject sets out the duty imposed upon a Member to send to the Institution within 28 days of the relevant request, a copy of his records of this activity.

The obligation arises under Rule 38(c), the breach of which will amount to a conduct offence.

(4) Professional Indemnity Insurance

Rule 9 of the Schedule provides for the obligation upon Members to provide evidence of their insurance cover to the Institution. The subject is discussed in much greater detail in Chapter 8.

It should be carefully borne in mind that the notification obligation is an immediate one in cases where the Member ceases to maintain appropriate cover. This is an example of a Member being required to communicate bad news to the Institution which may have the effect of bringing a disciplinary inquiry into play. Nevertheless, the position of the Member will be enhanced by co-operation. A very serious view will be taken of any failure.

(5) Accounts

This subject is discussed in much more detail in Chapter 4.

The notification obligation here is imposed by Rule 28 of the Schedule and relates to the obligation to deliver once in every period of 12 months a Certificate and/or Accountant's Report within six months of the end of the financial year.

These Certificates and Reports represent an essential part of the mechanism of self-regulation and compliance is essential so that the public may have confidence in surveyors who hold their funds.

(6) Imposition of fines by the Institution

This power derives from Bye-Law 22B and Rule 41.

Where a Member fails to deliver to the Institution any Certificate Report or other document required by any Bye-Law or Conduct Rule within a period of 28 days from the request for delivery, the Chief Executive has power to demand a fine by giving notice in writing to the Member.

The level of fine is £30 per week, or part of any week for the first four weeks (starting on any day) following expiry of the Notice that a fine will become payable if the required action(s) has/have not been taken, until the actions are fulfilled.

For the next four weeks or part of any week, the fine goes up to £50 and further increases to £100 per full week for all subsequent weeks.

These fines are payable within such period as is specified within the written Notice which period must be at least 28 days.

It is, however, common for breaches of notification requirements to be dealt with as matters of misconduct and dealt with according to the mechanisms set out in Chapter 3 on disciplinary structures and procedures.

(7) Self-preservation

The importance of proper communication with the Institution must never be under-estimated. There is often a tendency amongst professionals of all types to give priority to matters being dealt with on behalf of clients over and above the attention that is given to communications from their professional body. This inevitably leads to problems.

It can be said without flippancy that if a Member is really determined to find out all about the disciplinary process, then all he needs to do is to ignore correspondence from the Institution. Such failure leaves no real alternative to the Institution but to institute proceedings against the Member.

A failure to co-operate with the Institution is an example of conduct likely to result in expulsion in the absence of extenuating circumstances. This is particularly so where in the event of delayed communication, an attempt is made to mislead the Institution. All cases are of course dealt with on their own merits.

The aim of all Members must be to ensure that they never fall foul of any of these obligations either general or specific.

The 'ostrich' syndrome is wholly unacceptable. Behaving in this way does not mean that the problem will go away.

It means that the problem will get much worse. The syndrome described sometimes extends as far as failure by Members to even open letters addressed to them by the Institution. The potential pitfalls should be obvious.

Preventative measures will include the following.

- Always bear in mind your general duty to co-operate with the Institution.

- When letters are received from the Institution, open them and read them immediately.

- Treat such communications as matters of priority – do not put them aside until you find the time to deal with them.

- If you are irritated by the correspondence, for instance you consider a complaint is unwarranted, do not react by 'putting up the shutters' or being intemperate in your reply. Cool down and submit a measured response.

- Be careful to note the time limits imposed upon you by the Rules or by the Institution and comply with them. In cases of difficulty, write promptly to the Institution seeking an extension of time and setting out the reasons why this is required. The Institution will be reasonable in considering your request.

- Remember that telephone calls will not often suffice to discharge your obligations. By all means telephone the Institution in the first instance, but ensure that your response is put in writing as well.

- Remember that compliance with your various obligations is not as burdensome as it first seems. Most of the requirements are straightforward and will take little time. They pale into insignificance when compared with the consequences of failure.

- Be wary of delegation. Remember that you can delegate the work but not the responsibility which is yours at all times.

- Remember that the Institution is there to help you and sees the disciplinary process as a last resort. Help is at hand if you seek it and guidance can be obtained over the telephone.

- Where appropriate discuss your problems with other professional colleagues who may be able to view the matter objectively and provide you with helpful advice.

As with your duty to communicate with clients as discussed in Chapter 7, your duty to communicate with the Institution is a straightforward one. What can be described as the easiest route to disciplinary proceedings is also the easiest to avoid.

Relations with clients

For the business to thrive it is essential that a Member maintains good relations with his clients – this is a crucial area of professional practice.

Of course everyone will have an individual approach, bringing his own personality to bear. It is crucial to remember that in dealings with clients there are professional obligations as well as commercial considerations and the discharge of the latter should never compromise the former.

As a matter of law it will never be a defence to a disciplinary charge that the Member was obeying the instructions of the client. Professional obligations come first.

Similarly, it is not for a Member to decide unilaterally what is or is not in the best interests of the client. There is always the need to take instructions. If those instructions conflict with a professional duty, then the Member will not be able to continue to act.

The general standards required are referred to in Chapter 1 on Conduct Unbefitting where Rule 3 is set out. Particular obligations are those to act with integrity, honesty, openness, transparency and accountability.

It is fundamental to the client relationship that a Member should be able to give impartial and frank advice to the client free from external pressures which would weaken the independence of the practitioner.

Chartered Surveyors owe the duty of utmost good faith to their clients. Clients must be kept informed of all developments whether positive or negative, and compliance with the above core values should ensure that a Member is never guilty of conduct unbefitting with respect to his dealings with clients.

Where the requirements of a client conflict with the professional duties of a Member, then it is essential that the situation is explained to the client, preferably in writing.

It is, of course, absolutely fundamental that Members deal with their clients honestly. The client must never be misled and keep in mind that misleading can be the result of passive as well as active conduct.

These are the general duties owed to clients. The scheme of Bye-Laws and Rules, however, provide more specific examples of duties imposed upon Members in their dealings with clients and these will now be discussed individually.

Standard of service

Rule 4 provides that 'a Member shall in the performance of his professional work, the conduct of his practice and the duties of his employment provide the standard of service and competence which the Institution can reasonably expect'.

This requirement to work to the appropriate level of quality is self-explanatory, but it should be borne in mind that the obligation relates not only to technical work carried out for clients, but also the running of the practice generally. The duty extends to employed surveyors.

Of course it is impossible to provide a strict definition of an acceptable standard of service and competence.

The Institution receives many complaints of a service nature. In the course of an Investigation, the Institution will assess the adequacy of the service and in doing so, account will be taken of whether or not the Member has followed the terms of any relevant Practice Statements or Guidance Notes, all of which are available to the profession.

The Institution cannot however resolve issues between Members and clients which are essentially questions of professional negligence and therefore are matters of law.

It is often the case that where this Rule is breached, then there is also involved a breach of one of the other obligations which will be discussed below.

Notification of Terms of Engagement

Rule 8 provides that a Member 'shall provide written notification to his client or prospective client of the terms on which he is to act and shall inform his client in writing that a copy of the Member's Complaints Handling Procedure is available on request'.

This Rule does not apply where the client is the employer of the Member.

Terms of Engagement are a matter for each individual Member and they can of course vary particularly with respect to the type of work being carried out. There are, however, some provisions in the Terms of Engagement that are mandatory. The terms must include provisions relating to:

(a) fees;

(b) the payment of expenses; and

(c) the manner in which expenses and disbursements are to be calculated.

Professionals often complain that it is very difficult to specify fees at the outset of every transaction. The Rule does not call for a fixed fee to be stipulated and compliance can be achieved by an explanation of the method of fee calculation. In such an event, it is still considered desirable for an estimate to be provided. In circumstances where updating is required, then this must be carried out in writing.

Compliance with this provision acts very much in the interests of the Member. Fees are much more likely to be paid without difficulty where they do not come as a shock to the client. In the unfortunate event of litigation being required to recover fees, then the Member's position is infinitely stronger where he has complied with his obligation to notify Terms.

Aside from the question of fees, situations can arise where the terms upon which the Member is to act are varied as time passes. In such an event, there is a mandatory obligation upon the Member to provide written notification of the variation to the client.

Of course many clients are of long standing and Terms of Engagement will have arisen through prior notification and a course of dealing. In such cases, it is not necessary to issue full Terms with each retainer, but there is an obligation upon the Member in such circumstances to provide written confirmation to the client that the established Terms will continue to apply, unless contrary Terms will have been agreed with the client and of course confirmed in writing.

There is also an obligation upon a Member to act promptly in providing notifications of his Terms of Engagement and any variation to them. This is best dealt with at the commencement of each individual retainer.

When the Institution investigates service complaints, the Member is generally asked to supply a copy of the Terms of Engagement issued to the client so that the complaint can be explored in the context of the professional retainer that actually existed. If it transpires that the duty to notify Terms has been breached, then this is likely to provoke a disciplinary charge over and above any allegations arising out of the actual professional work itself.

Confidentiality

This is of course an absolutely fundamental duty.

Rule 9 provides that, with two exceptions, a Member shall keep confidential:

(a) the advice that he has given to his client; and

(b) information concerning his client's affairs.

The word 'client' includes a past client and a prospective client.

The only exceptions to this duty are:

(1) where the client consents to disclosure of information that would otherwise be confidential; and

(2) where disclosure is authorised by any legislation, Court Order, or in the course of giving expert evidence or other evidence, under Oath.

A breach of this obligation will be considered to be very serious indeed. Breach of this duty can involve a breach of a legal obligation as well as a conduct obligation. All the information that a Member discovers about a client in the course of a retainer is confidential.

The duty of confidentiality applies irrespective of the source of the confidential information obtained. The duty continues after the end of the retainer, or even after the death of the client, when the right to confidentiality passes to the personal representatives.

Where information is acquired on behalf of a prospective client, the duty is likely to arise even if there is no subsequent retainer at law.

Where at the outset of a matter, a Member foresees confidentiality problems, then they should wherever possible be discussed with the client before instructions are accepted.

Where a Member is required by law to disclose confidential information, then he may do so. However, even if the client has agreed, he should be notified in writing that the Member is going to have to divulge the information in question.

It is sometimes the case that statutory authorities will request information about clients, but will ask the Member not to tell the client. Here circumstances are infinitely variable, and the best possible course of action for the Member to take is to seek independent legal advice of his own before acting upon the request that has been made of him.

The common law duty of confidentiality as expressed in Rule 9 is an ancient duty binding upon professionals such as Chartered Surveyors. A more recent statutory expression of this obligation derives from the *Data Protection Act* 1998.

This is a specialist area calling for expert advice in the event of any uncertainty.

For present purposes, the obligation under the Act applies to anyone obtaining, recording, holding or disclosing personal data. The term 'personal data' is widely construed. It will apply to business information about a sole trader, there being no distinction under the Act between the sole trader as an individual and his business. The term can also cover information about partners and company directors.

Where such data is dealt with as above, it is subject to eight enforceable principles of good practice which say that the data must be:

- fairly and lawfully processed;

- processed for limited purposes;

- adequate, relevant and not excessive;

- accurate;

- not kept longer than necessary;

- processed in accordance with the data subject's rights;

- secure; and

- not transferred to any countries without adequate protection.

The importance of fulfilling this obligation cannot be overstated. Any breach may well also amount to Conduct Unbefitting. A Member in breach may be exposed to a liability for damages.

Confidentiality is the bedrock of the relationship with the client and in any case of doubt the Member must deal openly and frankly with his client. It is highly recommended that written instructions should be obtained before any disclosure of otherwise confidential information is made and preferably the client should approve the disclosure in writing and in advance of disclosure. The utmost care is required.

Timeliness in handling client's affairs

Rule 10 provides that a Member shall:

(a) act with due diligence on behalf of his clients or his firm's clients; and

(b) reply promptly to correspondence in so far as the correspondents may reasonably expect to be entitled to such replies.

It can immediately be seen that this obligation is linked to the standard of service obligation imposed by Rule 4.

Essentially the obligation is to get on with professional work expeditiously and be prompt in communication with clients.

This is an unfortunately fertile area for complaints and again the obligation is not capable of precise definition.

The key to compliance is to discuss with the client the likely time scale at the outset of the retainer. Where delays arise, as they inevitably will, then the client should receive an explanation – again in writing.

It is essential that a Member replies promptly to correspondence from his client and the same applies to responses to telephone calls and e-mails.

A Member is not obliged to tie himself down at the outset of a retainer with regard to the time limit for reply, and of course occasions will arise when immediate replies cannot be provided.

Without recommending the practice, it is the case that some Members will issue acknowledgement postcards immediately that a communication is received from a client. This will, of course, reassure the client that his letter has been received, but be careful not to include any confidential information on any such card.

Clients are entitled to expect their instructions to be dealt with promptly and effectively and it is wholly unacceptable for a Member to ignore communications from any client. Some clients are of course more demanding than others, and professionals tend to term them 'difficult'. Remember that your duties to all clients are identical.

In extreme cases, overly persistent communications from clients can impede the Member in the discharge of his retainer. Here, there is no objection to politely pointing out this difficulty to the client.

In the most extreme cases, correspondence from clients can be considered to be vexatious. If in doubt, the Conduct Section at the Institution will take a view on this for you and your duties will then not be the same as for the vast majority of client communications.

Situations can arise where nothing is happening. This may be entirely in the interests of the client, but in any event it is prudent to provide clients with regular progress reports. These will put the client's mind at rest. An explanation of any inactivity in the matter in question is wise.

The duty does not only extend to dealing with communications from clients, it applies to the actual discharge of the retainer. Again the term 'due diligence' is not capable of any precise definition and neither would an attempt at a definition be desirable. Each case will be looked at on its own merits.

Members are not obliged to accept instructions. As a matter of general conduct, they should only take on such instructions as they are able to accomplish effectively. So many conduct problems arise from the fact that a Member has taken on work in which he has inadequate expertise. These then turn into 'rogue files'. The Member has a psychological difficulty in dealing with them, and they seem always to retain their place at the bottom of the pile of outstanding work. This situation should never be allowed to develop. If instructions have been accepted unwisely, then it is far better for the Member to explain the situation to the client and direct him to a more suitable practitioner. An alternative is to pass the file to a colleague in the Member's own practice. This is another example of the link with Rule 4. A case in which a Member is not able to provide the appropriate standard of service will soon turn into a case in which the Member has not acted with due diligence – or possibly has not even acted at all.

As Members are free to accept or decline instructions, it follows that overwork will not amount to a defence to an alleged breach of this Rule. It may be mitigation but it is mitigation that Disciplinary Boards hear a great deal, and consequently as mitigation it lacks power.

Where clients feel ignored or neglected, then they are provoked to complain and disciplinary consequences are likely to follow.

Complaints Handling Procedures

Rule 11 imposes an obligation upon Members to operate a Complaints Handling Procedure.

The obligation applies to Members who are sole principals, partners or directors of a firm and who are offering surveying services to the public other than services provided only to the Member's employer.

The fundamental obligation is to ensure that the firm has, and operates, a formal procedure for dealing with client complaints and complaints from any person other than an employer to whom, in the opinion of the Institution, a duty of care is owed.

Persons to whom Members owe a duty of care will certainly include the following:

- any person to whom a duty of care is established by way of case law or statute;

- a person to whom advice is given and which gives rise to a special relationship between the Member and that person; or

- a person to whom advice is given where the Member intends the person to rely upon that advice.

It must be borne in mind that this list is not exhaustive. Even if a Member suspects that the person in question will rely upon the advice given, then a duty of care will arise. In any case of doubt, independent legal advice should be sought and the Institution will also help.

The Rule lays down a minimum requirement for any Complaints Handling Procedure which must be committed to writing. Unless a statutory scheme is being operated, the procedure must, as a minimum:

(a) state the name of the person with whom initial contact can be made;

(b) include a time scale both for the timely acknowledgement of the complaint and a time scale within which the Investigation will be completed;

(c) include reference to:

    (i) a right of the complainant to a separate review by an appropriately qualified person;

(ii) mediation where both parties agree; and

(iii) a right of the complainant, if still dissatisfied, to have the complaint referred to independent third-party decision.

If any client or member of the public requests a copy of the Procedure then it must be made available within 28 days. It is best practice to issue a copy by return.

Where the process has worked through and the complainant remains dissatisfied, then the Procedure must provide the complainant with a right to have the complaint referred to the Surveyors Arbitration Scheme, or any other scheme approved by the Institution under which complaints may be resolved quickly and with the least formality. The Member must ask the complainant in writing whether he wishes to use a scheme and if the complainant agrees then a referral must be made.

The Institution will be happy to provide Members with a model form of Complaints Handling Procedure, but Members may of course draft their own as long as it is compliant.

Procedures must provide for a brisk timetable, be clearly written and impartially implemented. The time scales set down in the Procedure have to be followed and complainants cannot be charged for work done in the operation of the Procedure.

The Procedure must nominate the first point of contact and, in the case of sole practitioners, it will be necessary to enlist the help of another possibly on a mutual basis.

Complaints can have insurance implications. They may include an element of potential negligence and insurers must be notified as soon as possible where potential arbitration or legal action arises. Notification to insurers does not absolve the Member from compliance with Rule 11.

Some practitioners consider this obligation to be onerous. However, the obligation contains an element of protection for the Member. If complaints are speedily and effectively resolved, the confidence of the client will often be maintained. Complaints will arise in the course of any practice, particularly a busy one, and speedy and cost effective resolution assists not only the complainant but also the Member. In particular, it is likely to avoid complaints to the Institution.

Again there is an overlap with the obligations with respect to standards of service and timeliness in handling clients' affairs. If the Institution is investigating a client complaint, it will generally advise the client to request the Member to disclose his Complaints Handling Procedure and the complainant will be urged to take advantage of it. If there is no procedure or a failure to disclose any such procedure that does exist, then disciplinary consequences are likely to follow. Many Members appearing before Disciplinary Boards would not have had the experience had they maintained proper procedures and utilised them effectively.

Some professionals of all descriptions seem to have an aversion to admitting mistakes or saying sorry. This syndrome is to be avoided. The obligation does not require a cumbersome, time consuming and expensive procedure – quite the opposite. The fulfilment of the minimum requirements is a most attractive alternative to litigation or disciplinary process.

Conflicts of interest

A conflict of interest includes any circumstance or potential circumstances:

(1) where the Member's interest is or could be in conflict with that of his client; or

(2) where two or more clients' interests or may conflict; or

(3) which are reasonably liable to be seen as interfering with the Member's objective judgement.

It is thus essential to note that we are dealing not just with actual conflicts but with potential conflicts which require a proper degree of foresight by the Member.

Objectivity is one of the core values and must always be maintained.

Where a situation arises in which two interests exist and the Member cannot do his best for both, then he may be said to be in a conflict situation.

It must be remembered that the term 'client' includes clients both past, present and prospective. The foreseeability of a conflict should therefore be assessed at the outset of a new retainer and should always be reviewed in the course of an existing retainer. As has been established with confidentiality, duties to clients do not expire with the termination of the retainer – quite the contrary.

The question of conflict is linked to the duty of confidentiality – see above.

Rule 16 provides that it is not a conflict where the Member's firm is a part of a group of firms and one firm in the group acts for one client and another acts for another client with conflicting interests, provided that:

(a) the firms are separate legal entities;

(b) there are no directors, partners or employees in common;

(c) there is no direct or indirect fee sharing between the firms; and

(d) there is no access to information or common internal data-sharing arrangements relating to the area of conflict.

Rule 17 provides that without prejudice to any other situation where a conflict of interest may arise, a conflict will certainly arise where a Member, his firm or associate, possesses confidential information concerning a past or existing client which may be of relevance to the interest of a new or prospective client, or to another existing client. Such information may not be used against the interests of that past or existing client save pursuant to any statute, Court Order, or in the course of giving evidence as an expert witness, or evidence under Oath.

This Rule derives from the common law duties of professionals. Members are under a duty to keep their clients' affairs confidential. On the other hand, Members are under a duty to communicate to their client all relevant information derived from whichever source. It can therefore be seen that these interests will come into collision. Rule 17 therefore deals with this specific situation and prevents use of the information.

Where the interests of a Member conflict with those of a client

Rule 18 deals with the situation where the interests of a Member conflict with those of a client. It does not impose a bar upon acting in this conflict situation.

The Rule also applies to an actual conflict or a potential conflict. It provides that in such circumstances a Member must consider whether or not he or his firm is prepared to act or to continue to act for the client.

Obviously that consideration must be honestly applied and a positive decision one way or the other is called for.

Should the Member continue to act then he must:

(a) disclose to the client at the earliest opportunity the possibility and nature of the conflict, the circumstances surrounding it and any other relevant facts;

(b) advise the client in writing to seek independent advice on the conflict; and

(c) inform the client in writing either that he and his firm are not prepared to continue to act for the client in this capacity or that he personally or his firm cannot act or continue to act for him unless thereafter:

(i) the client requests him to do so unconditionally; or

(ii) subject to specified conditions that the Member has put in place, arrangements for handling the conflict which the client has approved in writing as acceptable to him.

Conflict between the interests of clients

Rule 19 deals with the conflict of interests of clients and is in similar terms to Rule 18 but with the following distinctions:

(a) in reaching the initial decision, the Member must consider whether or not he or his firm is prepared to act for any or all of the clients whose interest conflict;

(b) the disclosure and advisory obligations apply to all the clients in question;

(c) the provision for acting with approval or subject to conditions requires the blessing of all clients in question.

Personal interests

Rule 20 provides that where a Member acts as agent for the sale or letting of real property owned by the Member himself or by his associate, or in which he or his associate have an interest, then the relevant facts must be disclosed to any prospective purchaser or lessee or, if they have instructed one, to their lawyer.

The term 'the relevant facts' includes the nature and extent of the interest.

Similarly, where a Member acts as agent for the sale of personal property owned by himself or his firm, then this must be disclosed to the prospective purchaser or representative. There is a separate provision with respect to farm quotas again calling for disclosure.

Public office holders

Rule 21 provides that where a Member holds public office which might lead to a conflict with the interest of any client, then there must be disclosure of the scope of the appointment to his client, and the client relationship must be disclosed to the public body by which he has been appointed.

Transparency of fees and benefits

By virtue of Rule 22, a Member must disclose to his client the nature of any fee, commission or other benefit that he stands to gain as a result of his appointment by the client other than that agreed with the client. This is to prevent secret profits being earned by the Member. Such profits are prohibited by law.

The situation generally

Where a surveyor is dealing with a conflict arising out of the confidentiality obligation (Rule 17) then he may consider it prudent not to act for the new client so as to avoid a breach of duty to the former client. There is, however, no absolute prohibition.

The fulfilment of one duty, e.g. a communication of all relevant information, cannot generally justify the breach of another duty, e.g. confidentiality.

The key to effectively dealing with conflicts is to recognise them in the first instance. If in doubt, legal advice should be taken or reference made to the Institution.

Essentially there will be two options open to the surveyor:

(1) to disclose the conflict as appropriate and obtain agreement as to how it will be handled; or

(2) to decline instructions which would involve a conflict problem.

If the Member decides to proceed to act, then the situation will need to be dealt with very carefully indeed. Conduct obligations will loom large and must be complied with. The Member will need to ask himself whether he is capable of effectively managing the conflict if this is what he proposes to do.

It is essential that when the conflict is disclosed, then this is done fully, clearly and in writing. When setting out the relevant facts be aware of the duty of confidentiality.

Any agreement obtained by the client should again be in writing and where appropriate should record the fact that independent advice has been obtained. Remember that this advice may not only be legal but also financial. It all depends upon the facts of the matter as to which independent advice is relevant. Bear in mind that more sophisticated clients in the commercial field may be in a better position to give informed consent than private individuals who may not have come across such a situation before.

If a conflict is capable of being managed, then it can be accomplished in two ways:

- if the conflict arises because of the Member's own interest, then it can be managed by proper disclosure of this to interested parties; or

- if it arises because of duties owed to different clients, it can be managed by the creation of a 'Chinese Wall' between those acting for the respective clients at your firm.

Great caution is advised if a Chinese Wall is established. They are notoriously difficult to properly manage and the law provides that any Chinese Wall must be sufficiently robust to offer no chance of information passing through it. This demonstrates the rigours of the requirement and will discourage many from the attempt. There is no defence of having taken reasonable steps.

The affected clients must agree to the Chinese Wall that has been arranged and, as a minimum, the Institution requires that:

- the individuals acting for conflicting clients must be different – this includes administrative staff;

- the individuals or teams must be physically separated at least to the extent of being on different floors of a building;

- any information, however held, will not be accessible to the other team at any time – documents must be held in separate locked accommodation to the satisfaction of the compliance officer or another senior person within the firm; and

- such compliance officer or other person must oversee the arrangement at all times and must be independent of the appointments concerned.

Furthermore, there will have to be appropriate education and training within the firm of the principles relating to the management of conflicts of interest.

It is suggested that small practices will find it virtually impossible to operate in this way. It is achievable within a large organisation, but the need for caution cannot be over-emphasised. The consequences of impropriety can be disastrous.

Members must bear in mind that when they act in breach of their obligations with respect to conflicts of interests, then clients inevitably feel betrayed and quite reasonably they will report what they perceive to be professional misconduct. In cases of any doubt or potential difficulties, it is thought more appropriate to decline the instructions and provide an explanation as to the reason why.

Self-preservation

This is a very wide area of professional conduct and some points of advice have been referred to above. The following is a summary.

- Remember the core values – if you comply with them you are unlikely to be in breach of any of the specific obligations.

- Only accept instructions which can be carried out within your own area of expertise.

- Do not accept instructions if you are simply too busy to take on any more work.

- Communicate with clients. Never leave them in the dark. Reply to letters and return their telephone calls.

- If you are in any difficulty in communicating adequately, then arrange to inform the clients of the reason. Do not encourage false expectations.

- Do not bury your head in the sand. Avoid the 'rogue file syndrome' at all costs.

- Where necessary seek the help of others and obtain advice from the Institution. Never assume that problems will simply go away.

- Have proper Terms of Engagement and communicate them to the clients at the outset. Both parties then know precisely where they stand.

- Maintain a proper Complaints Handling Procedure, make it available when required and utilise it properly. Seek the advice of the Institution who will provide you with a model form.

- Bear in mind at all times the paramount duty of confidentiality. Remember it can provoke a conflict of interest.

- Be very wary of adopting the Chinese Wall solution to a conflict. It rarely works.

- Never mislead and always communicate the bad news as well as the good news.

- Do not comply with instructions that lead you to breach your professional obligations which are paramount at all times. Explain this to clients and they will understand.

- Treat clients as individuals. They are all different and a one-dimensional approach is ineffective both commercially and professionally.

Professional indemnity insurance

Nobody is perfect. Everybody makes mistakes.

Even in the course of the most well-ordered practice, there will come a time where an allegation of negligence is made against a Member. It is essential for the maintenance of public confidence that Members are properly insured against such risks. Clients who have therefore been disadvantaged will be safe in the knowledge that they can be recompensed regardless of the financial position of the Member.

Accordingly, Bye-Law 19(6) provides that every Member shall in accordance with the Regulations be insured against claims for breach of professional duty as a surveyor.

This is a fundamental regulatory obligation. Failure to comply with the Rules is likely to threaten the Member's right to practise.

The Rules provide for minimum standards of compliance and confer upon the Institution the power to waive or modify in writing any provisions of the Rules – see below.

Rules 2–11 of Schedule 1 to the Rules of Conduct under Conduct Regulation 27.1 describe the detailed obligations.

Rule 3 provides that the insurance obligation applies to Members practising as surveyors or who are held out to the public to be practising as surveyors and who are:

- sole principals;
- partners;
- directors;
- consultants

to firms providing surveying services.

Therefore the Rules apply to Members described as 'Partners' or 'Directors' even if they are not properly described as such at law.

There are two exceptions. The Rules do not apply to Members who:

- work in the public sector;
- provide surveying services to their employers on an in-house basis and not to clients.

The Rules apply to your practising life and also for six years after you cease to practise – see below.

The obligation to carry insurance

Rule 4 imposes an obligation upon Members to ensure that they are adequately insured, at least to the extent required by the Rules, against any claims arising from work undertaken or performed within the United Kingdom, the Channel Islands and the Isle of Man.

Every Member must ensure that the cover extends to each partner, director, employee or consultant to such a firm and not only to himself.

Where a Member is practising solely as a consultant to a surveying firm and can show that the firm has adequate cover, then the Member is not under any separate obligation to have insurance of his own over and above that held by the firm.

Accordingly Members are obliged to have Professional Indemnity Insurance ('PII') when they are, or are held out to be, principals in private practice.

Employees undertaking private work for parties other than their employers will be treated as sole principals in respect of that private work.

The fact that the work done may not be the subject of charges is irrelevant. Free advice can attract claims.

Run-off Cover

Run-off Cover is the insurance cover that is required after a relevant Member ceases to practise.

Professional Indemnity Insurance operates on a claims-made basis. It is the policy in place at the time of the claim that is relevant and not the policy that was in place when the negligent work was performed.

As problems sometimes do not arise until much later, this type of insurance should be acquired.

Essentially cover is needed for at least six years after the Member last carried out any work. That does not mean that this period marks the end of the Member's liability which can extend to a fifteen-year period. Members ceasing to practise should, therefore, obtain specialist advice in this regard.

Rule 5 subjects a Member to a duty to ensure that any former sole principal, partner, director, employee or consultant of his firm, continues to be insured by that firm on an each and every claim basis against any claim arising from work previously undertaken, for a minimum period of six years from the date of cessation.

Where a firm becomes amalgamated, merged, dissolved, wound up or ceases to trade, then any Member who was or was held out to be a sole principal, partner, director or consultant of the firm must ensure that Run-off Cover is obtained for six years.

Where a Member is or was held out to be a partner, director or consultant in a firm where there was no other Member who was or was held out to be in any of the above positions and the Member leaves the firm, then he must arrange six years Run-off Cover with respect to his work, and work for which he was responsible at the time.

Where Members retired before 31 December 2001, the minimum limit of cover is £100,000 for each and every claim.

Where Members have retired on or after 1 January 2002, then the minimum limit is £250,000 for each claim. There is a specific provision for those who earned less than £50,000 annual gross income at retirement.

It can be seen that the above obligations are related to status. If the Member was an employee, then there is no general duty upon him to ensure that his work was covered by insurance, but certainly an employee should clarify the situation with his employer. If the Member is an employee but his employers are not Members, then the employee should obtain an indemnity from his employers against claims.

Employee Members remain personally liable for all the work that they do. They may thus be personally exposed if their employing firm ceases to trade and maintains no Run-off Cover.

The insurance requirement

The insurance requirement is set out by Rule 6 which details the minimum amount of cover for compliance with the Rules. In summary, the cover must be:

(a) £250,000 per claim where the gross income of the firm in the preceding year did not exceed £100,000;

(b) £500,000 per claim where the firm's income in the preceding year was between £100,000 and £200,000;

(c) £1m per claim where the gross income of the firm in the preceding year exceeded £200,000.

There are provisions for the permissible levels of uninsured excess.

Members must insure by means of a policy of insurance no less comprehensive than the form of the RICS Professional Indemnity Insurance policy in force at the time when the policy was taken out.

It should not be assumed that this minimum cover will be suitable. All will depend upon the type of work being carried out, and it may very well be the case that Members will require much more cover than the minimum level. That decision is commercial rather than a matter of conduct.

The Institution strongly recommends that insurance brokers are consulted with respect to the level of cover required.

Brokers will be able to make an accurate comparison between any insurance that a Member is about to acquire and the RICS policy in force. As ever, the Institution is anxious to be of assistance and will supply all necessary documentation and give appropriate advice.

Lack of appropriate insurance can lead to financial ruin and is viewed very seriously indeed by Disciplinary Boards. Failure to comply with these Rules is a frequent reason for expulsion. The public is perceived to be at risk and the reputation of the profession suffers drastically in such circumstances. Of course being expelled from the Institution for having inadequate or no insurance has no impact at all upon the position at Civil Law and Members should never expose themselves to an uninsured position. The insurance held will also cover according to the terms of the policy, the costs of defending any negligence action.

The Assigned Risks Pool

Professional Indemnity Insurance is purchased in the market. The Institution will provide details of insurers and brokers with the ability and expertise to assist Members in obtaining cover.

Occasions arise, however, where Members do not or can not obtain cover in the market place.

Accordingly, Rule 7 provides for the Assigned Risks Pool, which is a temporary insurance facility which arranges cover for Members who are unable to comply with the Rules because they have been refused cover. Entry into the Assigned Risks Pool is not automatic. Members must satisfy the relevant Rules of Admission.

Members should do all that they can to avoid falling into the Assigned Risks Pool. The premiums are likely to be very expensive, and failure to pay them is regarded as a conduct offence.

Once a Member is no longer eligible to remain in the Assigned Risks Pool, he resumes his obligation to obtain insurance through more orthodox means, but again may be faced with onerous premium requirements.

Listed insurers

The Institution maintains a list of approved insurers. Cover obtained must be with one or more of these insurers. A policy with any other organisation will not suffice to comply with the conduct obligation.

Monitoring and return of Certificates

The monitoring and return of Certificates is another example of a Member's duty to communicate properly with the Institution – see Chapter 6.

Rule 9 provides that a Member must provide to the Institution:

- a signed Certificate setting out details of insurance cover within 28 days of the policy coming into force; or

- within 28 days of being required to do so by the Institution, documentary evidence either that the Member is exempt from these requirements or that he has complied with them.

There is a further obligation upon Members who cease to have insurance to notify the Institution immediately. This may be considered somewhat unpalatable, but is essential for the maintenance of public confidence.

Rule 41 provides that the Institution has powers to impose fines for failure to deliver this information within 28 days of the request. The level of fine is £30 per week for the first four weeks, going up to £50 per week for the next four, and £100 per week for all subsequent weeks.

A more usual course of action in cases of insurance default is the instigation of disciplinary proceedings with potentially very serious consequences.

Exclusion of liability

Rule 10 prohibits a Member from holding insurance which excludes liabilities for previous claims, unless the exclusion is limited to claims arising as a result of work undertaken more than six years from the date on which the insurance was effected, or the same liability is covered by a separate policy of insurance.

As a general rule it is most unwise for Members to obtain a policy allowing any exclusions unless another policy covers the situation.

Waivers

If a Member wishes to obtain a Waiver from any of the insurance obligations, then an application must be made to the Institution and any Waiver granted must be in writing.

Rule 11 gives the Institution the power to grant a Waiver, with or without conditions, but the power is only exercised under exceptional circumstances, for instance but not exclusively:

- voluntary work for charities;

- working exclusively for one client.

Applications for Waivers are dealt with on their merits and it is not appropriate to lay down overly specific guidelines.

If, however, the uninsured practice has been for a relatively short period, and the position has since been regularised, a Waiver application may succeed if:

- the Member is able to declare that he has not been notified of any claims arising during that period; and

- the Member is able to produce letters of indemnity from all his clients releasing him from all liability during the period in question.

It must be emphasised that the circumstances in which Waivers are granted are rare indeed.

Self-preservation

This is a very specialist area and the content of this chapter has set out the basic requirements.

Accordingly, the following should be carefully borne in mind.

- Be aware of the expiry date of your policy. Do not depend on others.

- Always obtain specialist advice from reputable brokers.

- The Institution will be happy to provide you with details of brokers, insurers and RICS policy.

- Shop around in the market place for the most effective cover. You are likely to find that quotations vary quite dramatically between insurers.

- Do not allow your insurance to lapse in the process of seeking the best replacement cover.

- Remember your duty to communicate with the Institution which in certain respects does not depend upon the Institution approaching you in the first instance.

- The question of status is relevant and if you are in any doubt as to your position then seek advice from the Institution.

- Remember the obligation with respect to Run-off Cover and consider insuring yourself beyond the six-year period.

- As an employee you may be vulnerable. Ensure that you are aware of your employer's position so that you are not financially exposed to any claims.

- If you face disciplinary charges arising out of lack of insurance cover, remember that by far the best mitigation is that you have put your house in order by the time the matter comes to be heard. Failure to do so may well lead to expulsion.

Index